"I couldn't put it down."
— *Bradley Jenkins, guy whose hands were super glued to the book as the result of a cruel prank*

"Without a doubt, one of the best books that has ever been published in the history of the world."
— *Bonnie Shuttlesworth, mother of the author*

"A bit long for my taste so I didn't finish it. There were no pictures and the pages were much more dull than the glossy ones I'm used to reading."
— *Frank Frankerson, a man who's more into magazines*

"At no point during his rambling, disjointed writing does Ted Shuttlesworth Jr. ever arrive at anything that can be described as a coherent thought."
— *Guy Persons, Ted's critical neighbor*

"[Ted] tried to set up a table with his books for sale and after repeatedly asking him to leave we had to call the police to escort him out."
— *Juanita Sole, cashier at Benji's Books 'n' More*

Praise. Laugh. Repeat.

TED SHUTTLESWORTH JR.

Published in Virginia Beach, Virginia by Miracle Word Publishing.

Miracle Word titles may be purchased in bulk for educational, business, fundraising, or sales promotional use. For information, please e-mail info@miracleword.co

ISBN 978-0-9909196-0-5

Printed in the United States of America

*To my Dad and Mom who gave me
a love for reading and writing . . .
but not arithmetic.*

CONTENTS

*pose, so his plan is to rob you of strength so you can't
fulfill it.*

FOREWORD

....

Praise. Laugh. Repeat. is a powerful and humorous book that will teach you the winning basics of the Christian Walk.

If you understand and walk in these principles, you will build a solid foundation for your life, which will allow you to stand firm and weather the storms that come along. As you continue to walk in the truths of God's Word, you will realize that the circumstances of life, which normally would get you down and defeat you, will have no effect at all.

Remember that praise is warfare. Let God arise and His enemies be scattered! (Psalm 68:1) Laughter wreaks havoc in the camp of the enemy and will have him in confusion. As the Bible says in Job 5:22, "At destruction and famine you shall laugh!" The joy of the Lord is your strength! (Nehemiah 8:10)

The principles that Ted Shuttlesworth Jr. shares in

Praise. Laugh. Repeat. are simple, yet powerful. These profound truths will change your life.

It blesses me to see the next generation of the Shuttleworth family doing what God has called them to do. I am excited to see what the Lord is doing through Ted and what He will continue to do in the future.

Dr. Rodney M. Howard-Browne
Revival Ministries International
Tampa, Florida
October 2014

WINNERS DON'T CRY

···

"Weeping may last through the night,
but joy comes with the morning."
—PSALM 30:5

I ran across the platform, jumped into the air and landed a perfect flying kick into the chest of the man who was closing the service in prayer. The microphone flew out of his hand and he fell sprawling off of the stage and onto the ground below.

The people who were bowing their heads in prayer a moment ago were now staring at me with their mouths hanging open. It was silent in the sanctuary other than the man groaning and fumbling around to get up off of the floor.

Slowly, I raised one arm in the air and yelled in my Braveheartiest voice, "FREEDOM!" To my great surprise everyone in the room stood up and began cheering!

Okay . . . so maybe that never happened, but this was

playing in my mind like an epic film as I was standing on the platform watching that man close the service in prayer.

We just had a powerful service that night. People had been saved and healed. Not to mention those who had been delivered from depression, anxiety, fear, ADHD and suicidal spirits. We sang and rejoiced together. People were jumping, dancing and praising God.

The atmosphere was charged with victory . . . until Mister Cryface got the microphone. He began to remind everyone about all the problems and issues that they had faced as he sniffled and sobbed.

Some people feel like they haven't been touched by God unless they have burnt through three boxes of Kleenex and destroyed their mascara. (Hopefully it's only the ladies destroying the mascara.)

Needless to say, the atmosphere took a nose dive.

I understand tears of joy and thankfulness, but that's not what this was. This was the kind of crying that just focuses on your problems and creates an atmosphere of sorrow.

Winners don't cry. You know why? Victory is joyful.

I've never seen an NFL team win the Superbowl and then hang their heads and walk somberly to the locker room to discuss the past.

They are chest bumping, high-fiving, doing crazy

dances, pouring Gatorade on their coach and scream-
ing. It feels good to win!

Wherever you read of victory in the Bible, you will
see the corresponding action is always rejoicing.

When David became the king of Israel, he gathered
his elite troops to go and recover the Ark of the Cov-
enant. The Ark represented the power and victory of
God.

When the Israelites began their journey back into the
city of Jerusalem, they were very careful to bring the
ark back praising God. In fact, David got in front of the
crowd and began to dance before the Lord with all of
his might. He danced so hard that he looked crazy and
undignified (2 Samuel 6).

I'm sure he didn't have any smooth moves. He just
looked insane. His wife made fun of him later for how
she thought he had made a mockery of the kingdom.
What she failed to understand, however, was that he
was rejoicing because victory had returned to Israel.

All of Heaven rejoices over each sinner that repents
and enters the kingdom of God. A singular victory insti-
gates a Heaven-wide praise break! (Luke 15:7).

Winners don't cry.

As you search the Word of God you'll find that crying
is always tied to sorrow for sin, mourning for loss, or a
reaction to what the enemy had done.

Weeping is reserved for the absence of faith and of God. Probably one of the most famous scriptures in the New Testament is also the shortest verse of scripture, "Jesus wept." (John 11:35).

Even the people of that day saw Jesus weeping and misunderstood it.

They thought He was weeping because His good friend Lazarus had died. They pointed out how much love Jesus had for His dear friend.

But let's think about this for a moment. Jesus had just finished telling Lazarus' sister, Martha, to cheer up because He was the embodiment of resurrection power. Jesus was there for the sole purpose of raising Lazarus from the dead. So are we to believe that He was crying for the loss of a friend that He wouldn't see again until Heaven knowing that He was about to raise him back to life?

Maybe we're supposed to believe that Jesus didn't really know if He could raise Lazarus back to life, so He was crying in His insecurity. That cannot be true because when Jesus prays He boldly says, "Father, thank you for hearing me. You always hear me . . ." (John 11:41-42).

The reason Jesus wept in this passage was the same reason He was upset in His own home town when His miracle ministry was stifled. Unbelief.

Jesus is our prime example. Many times people paint

a picture of Him as though He was very somber and serious and downcast. While I believe He was serious about carrying out His ministry, I do not believe He was ever downcast. In fact, the Bible says He was filled with the joy of the Holy Spirit (Luke 10:21).

LAUGHTER FOLLOWS LIBERATION
SINGING FOLLOWS SALVATION

If you have gone to church for any period of time, you're familiar with the hymnal. If you're relatively new to church, you've probably not seen a hymnal. Hymnals are the song books that we used to sing from in church before technology gave us overhead projectors. This was back when people actually sang in church as opposed to scrolling their Twitter feed while someone performed worship sets on the stage.

Many of the hymns that were sung focused on the finished work of Jesus Christ and the benefits afforded to us as a result. Here's an example of a refrain written by Henry J. Zelley:

> *He brought me out of the miry clay*
> *He set my feet on the Rock to stay*
> *He puts a song in my soul today*
> *A song of praise, hallelujah!*

We were singing about how wonderful it is to be free from sin and on our way to Heaven. There is joy in serving the Lord! Look at what the Psalmist wrote regarding Israel being set free:

> *When the Lord brought back his exiles to Jerusalem, it was like a dream! We were filled with laughter, and we sang for joy. And the other nations said, 'What amazing things the Lord has done for them.'*
>
> *Psalm 126:1-2*

There are people in church all over the world who will tell you how hard it is to serve the Lord. They will tell you when you sign up for salvation you're signing up for a life of afflictions and trials. Just to sound spiritual they use a scripture, "Many are the afflictions of the righteous . . ." I wish they would finish reading because it says, "BUT the Lord delivers him out of them ALL!" (Psalm 34:19).

I believe if you're serving the Lord and it is extremely hard for you and you're always struggling, you may be doing it wrong. My reason for believing like that is because of something Jesus said regarding His way of living.

> *Come to me, all of you who are weary and carry heavy burdens, and I will give you rest. Take my yoke upon you. Let me teach you, because I am humble and gentle at heart, and you will find rest for your souls. For my yoke is easy to bear, and the burden I give you is light.*
>
> *Matthew 11:28-30*

I pray that this book will lead you into feather-light living for Jesus Christ as you learn to cast your cares upon Him. How? It's very simple. *Praise. Laugh. Repeat.*

PART 1

A NEW WAY OF LIVING

....

The days of riding the emotional roller coaster are over. Circumstances will no longer govern your happiness.

"As long as the devil can keep you from the realization of your new citizenship, he can also steal your benefits."

CHAPTER ONE

WELCOME TO A NEW KINGDOM

···

*"For the kingdom of God is not eating and drinking, but
righteousness and peace and joy in the Holy Spirit."*
—ROMANS 14:17

It's a wonderful thing to live a life of joy. Some people
spend their whole lives trying to discover happiness
only to find themselves completely frustrated because
they searched in all the wrong places.

It's important to understand that there is no natural
path to joy. I'm not talking about temporary happiness;
I mean real, lasting joy.

Happiness, though enjoyable, is fleeting. An event can
make you happy for a period of time. Seeing friends and
family can bring you moments of happiness. However,
when everyone goes home, is there a fountain within
you that continues to produce lasting joy?

Uncovering the fountain of joy is my reason for writing this book. It's not right for any believer to be afflicted

with depression, anxiety or fear. You are living in a new kingdom. The Apostle Paul made this very clear when he said:

> *For the kingdom of God is not eating and drinking, but righteousness and peace and joy in the Holy Spirit.*
> *Romans 14:17 NASB*

There are believers all over the world who are living for God, but they don't have any peace or joy. They are living in depression and anxiety!

Notice that if you are not experiencing peace and joy, you are missing out on two-thirds of God's kingdom!

You haven't just relocated into a new kingdom, you also have new benefits.

If you moved to the United States of America from another country and became a citizen, regardless of the laws of the nation you came from, you now enjoy the benefits afforded to you by the U.S. Constitution.

Maybe where you came from you couldn't express yourself with freedom of speech or worship with freedom of religion, but now, as a citizen of the United States, these rights belong to you.

The same is true in the kingdom of God. You are a citizen of a supernatural kingdom with supernatural benefits. As long as the devil can keep you from the realization of your new citizenship, he can also steal your benefits.

That is why knowledge of the truth is so vital to your new life in Christ. You can only experience what you know!

> *and you will know the truth, and the*
> *truth will make you free.*
> *John 8:32 NASB*

I want you to notice that it's not just truth that will make you free, it is the truth that *you know* that brings freedom. This is true in any circumstance. If you don't know what benefits are afforded, you will never take advantage of them.

A FIRST CLASS TICKET

I once heard a story of a man who had decided to move his family to the United States of America during the 1800s. The man made plans to relocate, begin working and save enough money to bring his elderly father to the United States to live with them.

When he had the money he needed, he purchased his father a ticket aboard a ship that would bring him to

America. The father received the ticket and with the little money he had, he purchased some cheese and crackers to eat during his journey.

He boarded the ship and began the voyage. Day after day the old man remained in his cabin and ate the cheese and crackers that he brought with him.

On one of the final days of the voyage the purser knocked on his door. When he answered the purser said,

"Hello, sir. I wanted to stop by and see how you've been feeling. The captain has been asking for you at every meal."

Embarrassed, the elderly man hung his head. "No sir, I feel fine. I just can't afford to pay for any of the meals, and that's why you haven't seen me there," he replied.

"I don't think you understand," the purser said. "May I see your ticket?" As the old man handed over his ticket the purser continued, "You have a first-class ticket, sir. All of your meals are included in the price of the ticket. You have a reserved seat at the captain's table. Please join us tonight, we're having steak and lobster!"

Many believers are living the same way in the kingdom of God today! Christ bought them a first-class ticket to Heaven when He died and rose again, but instead of enjoying the benefits, they are eating cheese and crackers until they get to Heaven.

You must know the truth of God's Word and the truth that you know will bring you into complete freedom. The Word of God will always bring you into a new revelation of life.

Look what the Psalmist wrote regarding the Word:

> *The entrance of Your words gives light; It gives understanding to the simple.*
> **Psalm 119:130 NKJV**

The only reason that any believer is living in darkness in any area is because the Word of God regarding that issue has not flooded their life.

GIFTS INSIDE A GIFT

It is very important to note that joy is a fruit that comes from the Holy Spirit. Joy is a spiritual thing that can only be spiritually attained.

Before Jesus left the earth He instructed His disciples to go to Jerusalem and wait there until He sent them power from Heaven in the form of the Holy Spirit (Acts 1:4-5).

The disciples were already Christians and had already preached the gospel, healed the sick and cast out devils, but Jesus knew that when His authority left the earth, they would need to be filled with the Holy Spirit just as He had been before His temptation.

The Holy Spirit is the One Who gives us power from Heaven to become like Christ. The fruit of the Spirit could be referred to as "the personality traits of Jesus."

We must have the power of the Holy Spirit to overcome the tendencies of our natural minds. Although your spirit is made new when you get saved, you still have the same mind and body. It doesn't matter how long you are a Christian, your mind will have to be continually renewed and your body will have to be disciplined for this reason:

> *The sinful nature wants to do evil, which is just the opposite of what the Spirit wants. And the Spirit gives us desires that are the opposite of what the sinful nature desires. These two forces are constantly fighting each other, so you are not free to carry out your good intentions.*
>
> *Galatians 5:17*

One translation says that your flesh is "at war" with your spirit. The power of the Holy Spirit is what gives you the ability to overcome the natural order of the earth.

Understand that there is not always a natural reason to be joyful, but we are still instructed to have joy. The enemy will work his hardest to steal your peace, but that is why the Bible says,

> *And the peace of God, WHICH SUR-*
> *PASSES ALL COMPREHENSION, will*
> *guard your hearts and your minds in*
> *Christ Jesus.*
>
> *Philippians 4:7 NASB*

The peace of God would not surpass comprehension if you were in a situation that warranted peace. It's not hard to be at peace when everything is going right. That's why the fruit of the Spirit are supernatural. They give you the ability to manifest the personality of Christ even when the natural world looks chaotic! The Holy Spirit is a gift from Heaven, the fruit of the Spirit are gifts inside that Gift.

Mark chapter 4 tells us about a time when Jesus and His disciples got on a boat and began a journey to the other side of the sea. After Jesus had fallen asleep in the back of the ship, a great storm arose and waves began to beat against the ship until it filled with water.

Jesus wasn't below deck in a sound-proof cabin, He was on deck sleeping through a severe storm! They actually had to wake Him up and ask for help. When Jesus woke up and saw the storm and the boat filled with water, He didn't panic. Jesus, full of the Holy Spirit, rebuked the storm and it obeyed Him!

Peace in the middle of an attack of the enemy is beyond comprehension in the natural realm. The same can be said for joy.

According to the Word of God there is a literal spirit of heaviness that is at work in the earth today (Isaiah 61:3). It actively seeks to weigh people down and bring them to a grinding halt.

When you are full of the Holy Spirit you are not subject to the cares of this world! You are a new order of mankind! You stand head and shoulders above the human species because part of the reality of the new creation process is that we dominate anything that opposes the Spirit of God on the earth!

> *For whatever is born of God overcomes the world; and this is the victory that has overcome the world—our faith.*
> **1 John 5:4 NASB**

We cannot afford to treat the mighty baptism of the Holy Spirit like a side item to the entrée of salvation! The mission of Jesus Christ was incomplete until He sent the Holy Spirit to indwell believers on the Day of Pentecost. Jesus said:

> *But I tell you the truth, it is to your ad-*
> *vantage that I go away; for if I do not go*
> *away, the Helper will not come to you;*
> *but if I go, I will send Him to you.*
> *John 16:7 NASB*

The Holy Spirit was not an option for the believers of the Early Church. Jesus commanded them to stay in Jerusalem until they were filled with power from Heaven.

As soon as Peter and John heard that the city of Samaria had received the Word of God and there were believers there, they immediately traveled to Samaria and laid hands on the believers and they were all filled with the Holy Spirit! (Acts 8:14-17).

We see the same thing take place when the Apostle Paul finds believers in the city of Ephesus. He was amazed that they had not been filled with the Holy Spirit. When he heard that they weren't, he laid hands on them and they were all filled with the Spirit and began to speak in a heavenly language and prophesy! (Acts 19:1-6).

Isn't it interesting that Paul didn't give them a seven-week series on being filled with the Holy Spirit and then have them fill out a card that let him know who was interested in taking next steps toward receiving Holy Spirit baptism?

He didn't even ask them if they would like to be filled with the Holy Spirit. He simply laid hands on them and they received.

It is God's desire for every believer to receive the baptism of the Holy Spirit so that they may access the power and benefits that are only to be found within.

WORK SMARTER NOT HARDER

When I was a teenager one of my responsibilities was to cut the yard at our house in West Virginia. We had an old lawn mower that I'm positive only started by the grace and mercy of the Lord.

I would push it over the grass of our property and up the steep hills of our back yard. When I was finished I would be tired, sweaty and covered in grass.

Years later, I went away to college and my father reclaimed the task of mowing the yard. Once, when I came back for the summer, I heard my dad cutting the grass, and when I looked out the window he wasn't pushing that old, beat up lawn mower around, nor was he sweaty or covered in grass. He was riding on a brand-new tractor sipping a glass of iced tea while he worked!

That's how it is in the kingdom of God. You can try to live for God on your own and sweat and get frustrated when the world is frustrated, or you can receive power in the Holy Ghost and do what you are called to do with ease as the force of Heaven's momentum backs you up!

> *For the kingdom of God is not eating and drinking, but righteousness and peace and JOY IN THE HOLY SPIRIT.*
> *Romans 14:17 NASB*

The key is found in this verse. Your joy will not be natural. You will receive and experience joy in the Holy Spirit! You will never be the same again in Jesus Name!

As you read this book you will uncover the fountain of joy in your life. Get ready to be filled with strength as you step into the best days you have ever known. It is time to take command in the supernatural realm.

....

"There are two invisible forces constantly pulling us into two very different predetermined destinies."

....

TWO PLANS
....

"The thief's purpose is to steal and kill and destroy.
My purpose is to give them a rich and satisfying life."
—JOHN 10:10

I was preaching just outside of Pigeon Forge, Tennessee, in 2013. One night, the Lord led me to preach on the joy of the Holy Spirit.

After I finished preaching, I began to minister to people around the altar. I noticed one young man and was impressed by the Spirit of God to pray for his deliverance. He looked no different than anyone else in the crowd, but I knew he needed the power of God to set him free.

I laid my hands on him and commanded the spirit of depression to loose him and let him go. With his hands raised he began to jump and dance.

When the service was over he came to the altar and told me his story. He was battling severe depression and was ready to take his own life. He was sure that suicide was the only way out of the pain that he was feeling.

When his parents left town just the week before the meeting he went into their bedroom and found his father's handgun. Sitting down on the edge of his parents' bed he raised the gun to his temple. With his finger on the trigger he prepared to take his life.

His cell phone rang.

He answered it with the gun still in his hand. It was one of his friends inviting him to come to the meeting that we were having.

He agreed to go, but he made up his mind that this would be the last thing he ever did. He would attend the meeting with his friend and then come home and kill himself.

Little did he know that the Holy Spirit would meet him there and bring deliverance and freedom to his life. The devil was too late to kill him! The Holy Spirit changed his entire life in just moments.

That is why the Psalmist declared:

> *A single day in your courts is better than*
> *a thousand anywhere else.*
> *Psalm 84:10*

God can do in five minutes what counselors and doctors can't do in five years.

DON'T CUT DOWN THE TREE. RIP OUT THE ROOTS.

The true source of depression and anxiety is not physical or mental, it is spiritual. While I'm thankful for those who are doing their very best to help the hurting, counseling and medication can only deal with the effects of the issue and therefore cannot bring freedom.

In order to be truly free we've got to address the root of the problem. In the same way that love, joy and peace are spiritually received, depression and fear are also spiritually received. Consider this verse:

> *For God has not given us a spirit of fear,*
> *but of power and of love and of a sound*
> *mind.*
>
> *2 Timothy 1:7 NKJV*

If God has provided power, love and peace through the Holy Spirit, then it is the devil who is attempting to attack us with the spirit of fear and anxiety. The enemy is doing his best to use depression to destroy an entire generation.

We must realize that the devil is not using depression against you so that he can merely steal your laughter. The devil doesn't care whether or not you laugh. There are a lot of people who laugh but are still secretly battling internally. That's why the Bible says:

> *Laughter can conceal a heavy heart, but when the laughter ends, the grief remains.*
>
> *Proverbs 14:13*

Our enemy's purpose is not to be a grinch and make sure that we have a bad day. We've got to realize that the devil has one desire — to destroy us. He is not satisfied until a generation is utterly destroyed.

In fact, he wants you to experience the temporary pleasure of sin. The Bible doesn't say that when you sin it will be no fun and you will hate every moment of it. The Bible speaks of the "fleeting pleasures of sin" in Hebrews 11:25.

If sin were not pleasurable there would be no temptation associated with it.

Sin is a seed and the fruit that it produces is death (Romans 6:23). The devil uses everything that he can to lead you not into unhappiness, but into death.

There are two external forces constantly pulling us into two very different predetermined destinies. A destiny of abundant life and another destiny of absolute destruction. This is what Jesus was talking about when He showed the contrast between Himself and the devil:

> *The thief's purpose is to steal and kill and destroy. My purpose is to give them a rich and satisfying life.*
>
> *John 10:10*

As we draw closer to the return of Jesus Christ, the devil is doing everything he can to expedite his plans. He knows that we are in the last days and have entered into the season of Christ's imminent return. That's why he's throwing everything he has at this generation.

As I was doing research for this book I began to think, *I don't remember my friends and classmates being on antidepressants and having to deal with issues like ADHD like the students of today.*

That's because our enemy is hitting harder than ever before. In fact, a recent review conducted by Dr. Wilson M. Compton and Associates from the National Institutes of Health showed that major depression doubled in just one decade at the turn of the century.[1]

No matter how badly the enemy wants to destroy us, the power of the Holy Spirit is greater than any attack he may devise. Jesus is actively pulling us into the destiny that He has planned for us by the power of His

Spirit.

It's dangerous to just take life as it comes. Not everything that happens to us comes from God or because God designed it. When you realize that the devil has a plan of attack and that God has empowered you to assume control and fulfill your divine destiny, your eyes are opened to what is really going on in the unseen realm.

There is a war being waged for the souls of our generation. We can either allow ourselves to go with the flow and see where we end up, or take command of our future and align ourselves with the plans of God for our lives.

That's why when I see people being attacked by anxiety, depression, panic attacks and ADHD, my heart goes out to them. I treat these things like mortal enemies because ultimately that's what they are.

When Jesus dealt with sickness and bondage in the Bible, He always treated it as an enemy. He took control and commanded it to leave.

You'll never find a place in Scripture where Jesus told the suffering that it was His will for them. He never told anyone that it was for their good so that they could be a more faithful follower, a stronger believer, or a more pious person.

He simply healed them.

THE NURSE WHO QUIT

One summer, I was preaching at a camp to a group of students. During this particular service I was ministering on how the power of the Holy Spirit can set you free from depression, anxiety attacks and ADHD.

I shared with the students that the Bible says God is a "jealous God" (Deuteronomy 6:15). This simply means that He wants all the glory, honor, praise and worship.

This is why when He touches you with His miracle-working power, He does so in a way that shows His greatness.

God doesn't want to do something so small in your life that it could be swept under the rug or ignored by men. On the contrary, God wants to be praised for His mighty acts of greatness (Psalm 150:2).

I was teaching these students that they could be healed of depression and other issues and never have to take medication again. I told them that it was not God's will for them to be on medication and they could be free and healed.

Apparently, one of the nurses at the camp did not agree. I found out later because after that service she marched into the camp offices, turned in her lanyard and went home.

When she got home she was still upset enough to

write me an eight-paragraph rebuke on Facebook. (I actually prefer to receive my criticism on Facebook because instead of having to stand there and listen to the person drone on and on, I can quickly scan the message and then reply, "LOL.")

She proceeded to tell me that, "faith and prayer are good things to have in your life, but these kids need their medication!"

God doesn't need the assistance of doctors or medication to bring healing and help to His children. Faith and prayer are not just nice extras to have at your disposal, but keys that unlock the blessings of Heaven!

The nurse's response is a dangerous way to think and conduct your life. Putting God on the back burner and relying on the strength of man's wisdom might work for you when you have an annoying little cold, but what do you do when it's cancer?

What do you do when the doctors shake their heads and tell you they're sorry but there's nothing more they can do?

We must place value on the destiny laid out for us by Christ. We will attain miracles by sticking to the methods found in God's Word.

It's not enough to just know that God has great things planned for your life (Jeremiah 29:11). You've got to actively pursue them. The plan of God doesn't just automatically function in the life of every believer. It has to be attained by faithfully seeking after it even in the small, everyday aspects of obedience to God's Word.

Dwight L. Moody, the great American evangelist, once said, "There are many of us that are willing to do great things for the Lord, but few of us are willing to do little things."

Joy is part of God's plan for your life. Don't surrender what God has set aside for you, assuming that whatever comes to you in life must be His desire.

Depression and anxiety are demonic attacks of the enemy and should be regarded with a righteous indignation. Refuse to be harassed by the devil.

God gave Israel a very interesting proposal in the book of Deuteronomy when He said, "Now listen! Today I am giving you a choice between life

> **THERE ARE MANY OF US WILLING TO DO GREAT THINGS FOR THE LORD, BUT FEW OF US ARE WILLING TO DO LITTLE THINGS.**

and death, between prosperity and disaster . . ." (Deuteronomy 30:15).

That choice is still laying in front of you. You stand at a crossroads today. Down one path lies disaster and destruction, however, the other path is filled with the wonderful blessings of Heaven. Let God lead you into the future He created for you.

....

"Whatever is not permitted to harass Jesus Christ is not permitted to harass you."

....

CHAPTER THREE

THE UNTOUCHABLES

....

*"For he raised us from the dead along with Christ
and seated us with him in the heavenly realms
because we are united with Christ Jesus."*
—EPHESIANS 2:6

My airplane touched down at John F. Kennedy International Airport in New York City. When the captain
turned off the fasten seat belts sign I grabbed my car-
ry-on baggage and filed out of the plane with everyone
else.

Inside the terminal I grabbed some lunch and kept
walking toward my next gate. I had been traveling for
quite awhile and I was exhausted, so when I saw the
V.I.P. lounge on the second level I was immediately interested.

I stepped on the escalator which let me off right in
front of the lounge. The dark wood, stainless steel and
blue accent lighting of the entrance basically said, "The
people in here are having more fun than you are out

there."

I had been in lounges like that before. I knew that once you got inside you are in a veritable promised land of good food, soft reclining chairs and possibly unicorns and the beginnings of world peace. The overcooked burgers and sodium-covered french fries in the bag I was holding no longer sounded so good.

I wanted to go in.

The only issue was the smug face of the snooty attendant working the desk outside the door. When she said, "May I help you?" It sounded more like, *"Move along. You obviously don't belong inside the lounge."*

WHAT CANNOT HARASS CHRIST CANNOT HARASS ME.

After talking to her I found out that in order to go in you had to have a certain loyalty credit card. I pulled out my wallet and began showing her different cards.

Apparently the cards that I had weren't impressive enough to allow me access. (She even rejected my Sam's Club and Blockbuster cards.)

It didn't matter what I did, I couldn't get inside. Even if someone in the lounge had come out to talk to me, once they went back inside I no longer had access to them.

This is the exact same thing that happened to you

once you received Jesus Christ as your Savior! There may have been a time when the devil had admission to your life, but now you are sitting in a place where the devil has no ability to gain access to you any longer.

You have become untouchable.

Standard religious thinking would have you believe that until we get to Heaven there is nothing we can do but go through the trials of life when they come.

The work of Christ, however, accomplished much more than that. He didn't die so that we could be worthy to live in survival mode. He died and rose again to elevate us into a place of power and authority.

> *For he raised us from the dead along with Christ and seated us with him in the heavenly realms because we are united with Christ Jesus.*
>
> **Ephesians 2:6**

Your enemy doesn't have the credentials to gain access to the heavenly realms. You are literally seated in a place that he wishes he could gain admittance to, but never can. I want you to say this phrase out loud. Memorize it, write it down and never forget the principle.

What cannot harass Christ cannot harass me!

ONE CHAMPION. BILLIONS OF BELTS.

The Apostle Paul told the Roman Church that we as believers are "more than conquerors through Him who loved us" (Romans 8:37 NKJV).

This phrase always confused me. How do you become more than a conqueror? If you have conquered then you are at the highest level because no one can defeat you. What more is there than that?

I heard R.W. Schambach, an evangelist who had a powerful healing and deliverance ministry, tell a story that explained this mystery perfectly.

Imagine a boxer who is preparing for the championship fight. He has trained and gotten himself into prime shape for the bout. On the night of the fight he marches into the arena and steps into the ring.

When the officials ring the bell the fight begins. The two boxers dance around the ring throwing punch after punch. Both boxers take punches and break the skin. It's possible that noses get broken and eyes are swelling.

Finally, one boxer throws the final punch knocking the other unconscious. He's down for the ten count. The officials ring the bell, grab the boxer's arm and hold it in the air signaling that he is the champion.

They bring the belt out and the champ drapes it over his shoulder as those in his corner shout and jump. The crowd is going wild.

But we all know that boxers don't fight for a belt, ultimately they fight for the money. So the winner receives the payout check for his victory. After showering and changing back into his street clothes, he begins home.

When he arrives at his house and walks in the front door, he finds his wife waiting for him. When she looks at him she's looking at the conqueror. He's been punched, bruised and hurt . . . but he is the conqueror.

Now the wife holds out her hand and the boxer reaches into his bag and pulls out the check. He puts it in her hand. She just became MORE than a conqueror. She never had to fight, take one punch, have her nose broken or break a sweat; but she gets to spend the check!

This is exactly what happened through Jesus Christ! He was beaten and bruised, He was crucified, He died and was buried and He rose from the dead . . . but now you get to enjoy His Victory!

> *But thanks be to God, who gives us the*
> *victory through our Lord Jesus Christ.*
> *1 Corinthians 15:57 NASB*

Redemption is powerful. It placed you on the heavenly level. You have become a new type of being. What kind of new species are you?

The God kind.

I'M JUST LIKE MY FATHER

Bedtime in our house is one of my daughter's favorite times because she loves to hear stories. Every night she picks out two or three books that we're going to read before she goes to sleep.

One night she picked out a book that told the story of a lion who was taken in by a herd of antelope when he was a cub.

They raised him year after year to be just like them. The lion ate what the antelopes ate and lived where they lived. They always told him to be careful because there were fierce creatures called lions in the wild that were very dangerous. So the lion lived cautiously day after day hoping and praying that he never came into contact with a lion.

One day, as the antelopes and the lion were eating, the lion lowered his head toward the water to take a drink. Looking down he saw his reflection and roared in fear. He quickly warned the antelopes that there was a lion in the water.

Sadly, the antelopes realized that they couldn't keep the truth from the lion any longer. They explained to him what he was. The story ends with the lion realizing his identity and happily reuniting with the pride.

The same seems to be true with many believers today. They're living on this earth as though they are still mere humans hoping that they don't fall into the crises of life. They don't even realize that they are a completely different species of being!

Let this thought process rearrange the way you see yourself in the kingdom of God.

> *But as many as received him, to them gave he power to become the SONS OF GOD, even to them that believe on his name:*
>
> *John 1:12 KJV*

When a dog has offspring they are always puppies. You will never find a dog giving birth to kittens. Lions have lions and human beings will always produce other human beings.

The Word of God teaches us the same is true of God. When He produces offspring He reproduces of Himself. Sons of God are on the God Level.

> *I say, 'You are gods; you are all children of the Most High.*
>
> *Psalm 82:6*

Jesus reiterated this very thought as He claimed to be the Son of God and it so angered the people they picked up stones to kill Him! (John 10:22-38).

We are new creations at the moment of salvation! The Bible doesn't say that we become *spiritual,* it says we become living spirit beings!

> *That which is born of the flesh is flesh, and that which is born of the Spirit is spirit.*
>
> *John 3:6 NASB*

A common misconception is that eternal life begins when you get to Heaven. This is simply not true. The moment that you receive Jesus Christ as your Savior you are recreated internally and you begin your eternal life.

We must begin viewing ourselves as God views us. He recreated us. He raised us to new life. He seated us in heavenly places with Jesus Christ. We are reigning from that position today.

I once heard a minister say that it is laughable to imagine Jesus living on the earth depressed and anxious. Can you imagine your Savior struggling to find a job or keep His marriage together? No. That is because there is a higher realm of living: the God Level.

The origin of the human race is the likeness of God. It was God Who decided to create us in His image and likeness (Genesis 1:26). It is no more blasphemous to see yourself on the God Level than it would be to consider yourself a child of your earthly parents. They produced you which secures your connection to them forever!

No matter how you may try, you cannot extract their DNA from your body. It is impossible. In the same way, you are a new creature formed with God's own DNA. When you know that truth, it will set you free.

THE FAUCET GETS WET FIRST

Why am I telling you all of this? I thought we were talking about joy here. We are! When you finish reading this book, I don't want you to just have joy, I want you to be empowered to break the curse of depression off of someone else. I want you to become what Christ is: a proactive wrecking ball to the kingdom of darkness.

However, not everyone is qualified to help others. This is the reason that no one reading this book has ever taken investment advice from a homeless person. Why? They are in no position to help you.

Bishop David Oyedepo is the senior pastor of one of the world's largest churches, Winner's Chapel. The church is located in Ota, Nigeria, where they host four packed Sunday morning services in their 55,000 seat auditorium. I heard him make a statement once that I will never forget.

"Only changed people can change the world."

When you go to your sink to pour some water in a glass, it is impossible to fill the glass with water and not get the faucet wet. The faucet, which brings the water to you, is the first element to experience the effects of the water.

The anointing of God that passes through you to benefit this world should benefit you first and foremost! You will never see someone bogged down with chronic depression making people double over with laughter.

You cannot give what you do not have. It takes an overwhelming, overflowing joy to bring deliverance to someone else. If it doesn't spill out of you it can never saturate them. It would be impossible to lead someone somewhere that you have never been! How would you describe the route to them?

I want you to see how arrogant the devil must be to think that he can harass you whenever he wants. The only power that the devil has over any believer is the power they give him! This is why the Apostle Paul instructed the Church in Ephesus to not give any place or position to the devil (Ephesians 4:27).

This proves to you that you can draw a line in the sand and tell the devil right where to stop. He is forced to obey your commands just as if it was God Himself speaking!

> *Submit therefore to God. Resist the devil*
> *and he will flee from you.*
> *James 4:7 NASB*

This verse shows us two things. First, the prerequisite to carrying God's authority is being submitted to God. All authority in the kingdom of God is delegated. The fact that a Roman centurion recognized this principle in Matthew chapter 8 blew Jesus away!

This is why unbelievers cannot rebuke the enemy of their soul. He is not required to obey them because he is in authority over them. When you submit yourself to God, however, you gain God's authority.

Secondly, this verse says to *resist* the devil. The Greek word that is translated "resist" here literally means to "stand in opposition." You cannot be satisfied with the attacks of the enemy in your life.

One summer afternoon, I was in my back yard grilling hamburgers. The people who lived next door owned a beautiful, big, white dog named Roxy. She would stand up on the fence and whine until I would come over and pet her.

That afternoon as I was grilling burgers, I walked back through the sliding glass door into my kitchen to grab some more marinade for the grill. When I turned to go back outside, I saw a white streak shoot through my house! I walked around the corner and looked down my hallway and there was Roxy sitting in my entryway panting and smiling at me.

It didn't matter how much I loved dogs, Roxy wasn't my dog and she didn't belong in my house with her muddy paws.

I walked down the hallway and took her by the collar and began to lead her back the way she came in. She did not want to leave. She dragged her hind legs the entire way. It didn't matter to me how much she wanted to stay, she wasn't staying in my house.

I took her back through the sliding glass doors and outside into the yard. When we got to the fence I lifted her up and placed her back into her yard. As I let her go I heard the Lord say, "That is exactly what you've got to do with the devil."

I knew what He was saying. There are those who have left the door to their life open and the enemy has run inside. Now he's sitting in their house smiling at them as though he belongs there. You have to get bold enough to grab him by the collar, drag him out the way he came in and kick him back where he belongs! Don't give place to the devil.

Finally, this verse says that the devil will flee from you. The word "flee" in the Greek language brings an amazing light to this verse. It is from the word *pheugo-mai*, which from the earliest times of Greek literature meant to flee or to take flight.

It was used to depict a lawbreaker who flees in terror from a nation where he broke the law. The reason he flees so quickly is that he wants to escape the prosecution process. Remaining in the nation would most assuredly mean judgment; so rather than stay and face the consequences, the lawbreaker flees for his life.

The devil is illegally harassing you! Today is the final day of your struggle with your enemy and his counterfeit power. He must leave you alone!

What is not permitted to harass Jesus is not permitted to harass you!

PART 2

ACCESSING OVERWHELMING JOY

·······································

*You cannot simply choose to have joy.
You must decide to walk the paths
that lead to joy.*

"Voice-guided commands from the Holy Spirit will lead you into the hidden blessings of God."

CHAPTER FOUR
SUPERNATURAL GPS

··

"You will make known to me the path of life;
In Your presence is fullness of joy;
In Your right hand there are pleasures forever."
—PSALM 16:11

I was lost again. In my own home town. I have a terrible sense of direction, which is crazy for someone who travels around the country for a living.

I was getting ready to make the dreaded phone call to my wife, who, by the way, has an excellent sense of direction. Now I was going to have to hear it all over again.

So the following Christmas, my wife bought me a GPS for the car. One thing I do know is technology, so I immediately went outside to install it. I chose the British female voice setting so that I could pretend to be James Bond when I was driving and took it for a spin.

You're probably familiar with how the GPS system works. You type in your desired destination point, hit "enter," and it calculates the fastest route to get there.

As you're driving, the GPS will give you voice-guided commands when it's time to make the next turn. Nobody in their right mind purchases a GPS, types in the destination and then disregards all the prompts from the machine. You will never reach your destination by ignoring all of the directions.

Can you imagine how foolish you would sound when your GPS gave you a voice prompt if you yelled, "You're just trying to manipulate me! You don't know where I need to go!"

Yet, people are missing out on overwhelming joy because they refuse to take voice-guided commands from the Spirit of God.

The Bible says this regarding the Holy Spirit:

> *When the Spirit of truth comes, he will guide you into all truth. He will not speak on his own but will tell you what he has heard. He will tell you about the future.*
>
> *John 16:13*

God is not giving you instructions because He wants to manipulate you. He knows how to lead you into overwhelming joy and peace!

God knows that if He can instruct you and you will obey Him, He has the ability to release to you the overwhelming joy of His presence and the pleasures that are in His right hand. This scripture is the basis for our first access point to overwhelming joy:

> *You will make known to me THE PATH*
> *OF LIFE; In Your presence is fullness of*
> *joy; In Your right hand there are plea-*
> *sures forever.*
>
> *Psalm 16:11 NASB*

God doesn't want you to be confused about where to go and what to do. He wants to make the path of life known to you.

Notice this verse doesn't say the "paths" of life. That is because God doesn't have a Plan A, B and C for your life. He has a singular plan and purpose for you. When you discover it and attach yourself to it, overwhelming joy belongs to you.

DON'T OVER DO IT. DON'T UNDER DO IT.

The key that draws the force of Heaven's blessing into your life is simple obedience. This is they same key that urged Jesus to perform His first miracle even when He said that His time had not yet come (John 2:4).

In that story Mary, the mother of Jesus, essentially tells the servants to do nothing more and nothing less than what Jesus commands them to do.

Stop.

That is the key. Don't do more and don't do less than what the Spirit tells you to do.

When you do more than God commanded you to do, you will wear yourself out and become frustrated. The Word of God declares,

> *Unless the Lord builds a house, the work of the builders is wasted. Unless the Lord protects a city, guarding it with sentries will do no good.*
>
> *Psalm 127:1*

If God isn't in it, it's not worth doing. I would rather operate with the force and momentum of His hand than attempt things on my own and hope they succeed.

This is how God took us effortlessly into our radio ministry. I was minding my own business and relaxing one afternoon when I received a call from a friend. He wanted to know if I would be interested in going on the radio. I told him that I would pray about it.

The very next day a pastor from a completely different part of the country called and asked me the exact same question! These two men didn't know each other, but God was using them both to guide me into my next step of ministry.

He explained that there was an opening on the largest Christian radio station in New England and they were looking for Pentecostal ministers to air. I knew this was confirmation and I received the Lord's direction that this was His next step for our ministry.

I called the first friend back and told him that I would be happy to go on the radio as soon as possible. When I asked him how much it was going to cost he said that it wouldn't cost me anything because he was going to pay the bill personally!

Shortly after that I was holding a revival outside of Charlotte, North Carolina. I announced the testimony of how God had opened the doors for us to go on the radio in these cities and reach a potential audience of over ten million people with the gospel every day.

That night, at a restaurant, I received a message on my phone from a minister I know. He had heard we were going on the radio. He asked me how much it cost to be on the radio each month in Boston. When I told him, he asked me to send my bank account information because he was going to wire enough money to pay the first two months of broadcasts!

The very next night, a woman in the meeting approached me after the service and asked how much it cost to be on the radio each month. When I told her she wrote a check and paid for another month of broadcasts.

Then, we received a phone call from another individual who had heard the news that we were beginning our ministry on the radio and wanted to pay for the fourth month of broadcasts!

I hadn't even produced, let alone aired, one program, but within a few days God had provided the first four months paid in full. Why? Because we were following His instructions and not our own desires. Jesus makes this way of doing things very clear when He says to His disciples:

> . . . *WHEN I SENT YOU out without money belt and bag and sandals, you did not lack anything, did you?" They said, "No, nothing.*
>
> *Luke 22:35 NASB*

When we receive supernatural instructions from God and obey them, we are swept into the current of overwhelming joy and peace! The burden of production is shifted from our shoulders to God's.

#SUBURBANCHRISTMASPROBS

Instructions are so important to you receiving God's best for your life. Probably one of the greatest enemies to following instructions is pride.

Abraham Lincoln once said, "What kills a skunk is the publicity it gives itself." We cannot lead lives that are filled with pride and succeed. Many men deal with the "I'm-the-man-syndrome." It has happened to me every Christmas since my daughter was born.

Each December I will go out to the store and buy all of her toys. Some of them I put together on Christmas Eve so that when she opens the boxes on Christmas morning she can immediately begin playing with them.

So late each Christmas Eve, I take the new toy into my living room, open the box with my knife and dump all the pieces onto the floor. What is the first step I take? I grab the instruction booklet and toss it over my shoulder.

I don't need that! I'm the man! I can rewire gadgetry, program my DVR and make a frozen pizza while tweeting and posting to Instagram each step of the way.

So the process begins. I start fitting the pieces, one after another, popping things into place that may or may not fit. After accidentally jabbing myself with the screwdriver and resisting the urge to demolish the whole toy with a flaming sledgehammer, I finish the project.

The problem, however, is that after I'm done I still have too many pieces left over and although the batteries are installed none of the lights in the toy turn on.

It's at this moment as I'm pointing a loaded .357 magnum at the newly assembled toy and armed with my Dirty-Harry-make-my-day-face that my wife comes in and gently suggests that maybe I should have looked at the instructions.

After about thirty minutes of reworking the toy, it finally fits together with no extra pieces. The lights are now flickering and even the sounds are playing.

I could have saved myself a lot of time and tons of frustration if I had just started the project with the instructions in hand.

Some people are confused as to why their lives are in pieces and they are struggling to make things work, but they have refused to accept the instruction of God's Word and His Spirit.

THE LORD IS MY SHEPHERD?

Even people who don't go to church can quote some portion of Psalm 23. They've heard it in some movie or song somewhere. The questions is, have we really looked into it? Do we understand the reality of it?

I want to draw out two key phrases from that Psalm to show you the power of the Shepherd who guides you.

First, David says,

"He makes me lie down in green pastures."

In his extremely insightful book, *A Shepherd Looks At Psalm 23*, Phillip Keller makes these statements;

> The strange thing about sheep is that because of their very make-up it is almost impossible for them to be made to lie down unless four requirements are met.
>
> Owing to their timidity they refuse to lie down unless they are free of all fear.
>
> Because of the social behavior within a flock, sheep will not lie down unless they are free from friction with others of their kind.
>
> If tormented by flies or parasites, sheep will not lie down. Only when free of these pests can they relax.
>
> Lastly, sheep will not lie down as long as they feel in need of finding food.

They must be free from hunger."[2]

We must understand that it is the Shepherd who knows where the green pastures are. If we are not willing to obey His prompting then we are not qualified to receive His provisions.

Secondly, I want you to understand this phrase:

"He restores my soul."

The enemy would love to do anything that he can to keep you dejected. He would love for you to remain cast down. In another passage David asks himself a question:

> *Why are you cast down, O my soul? And why are you disquieted within me? Hope in God . . .*
>
> *Psalm 42:11 NKJV*

Keller draws another comparison with the Psalm and shepherding, noting the significance of a "cast" sheep:

"This is an old English shepherd's term for a sheep that has turned over on it's back and cannot get up again by itself."

That is a powerful thought. Only through the instructions of our Shepherd can we be removed from an irreversible situation and brought into a place of comfort, peace and overwhelming joy. Obedience to God's instructions brings supernatural restoration of your soul.

Prayer gives us direct access to the instructions of God. He already has designed His plans for your life (Jeremiah 29:11). The key is to ask Him and uncover the mysteries of your future! (Jeremiah 33:3).

1.14.16

3 Call to me and I will answer you and tell you great and unsearchable things you do not know!

WOW, WOW, WOW.

3:33 - I am in here come to "Know" that God wants me to ask him for direction, but I never knew this was true scripture. 49 I need to read every word in the Bible ♡

#PraiseLaughRepeat

....

"The moment you become too busy to pray, you're too busy to live an overjoyed lifestyle."

....

CHAPTER FIVE

DEDICATION = DESTINATION

··

"Ask, using my name, and you will receive,
and you will have abundant joy."
—JOHN 16:24

The year was 1990. *The Fresh Prince of Bel Air* was premiering on TV. Bill Parcels and Lawrence Taylor were about to lead the New York Giants to a Superbowl Championship. Macaulay Culkin was starring in *Home Alone*, a movie that would annoy Americans for years to come. Stonewashed jeans, neon colors and L.A. Gear sneakers were cutting-edge fashion items.

When the holiday season came around, however, there was only one thing on the minds of young men like me. Something so life-changing that it was sure to alter the nature of our existence forever.

Super Mario 3 was being released for the Nintendo Entertainment System. You remember. The gray cartridges that you had to blow on and smack a specific number of times before they would work properly.

If there was a must-have that Christmas season, this was it. Super Mario in all his 2D glory, flying around the screen with his raccoon tail and ears.

I wanted it and so did all my friends. At eight years old, I didn't believe in Santa Claus, but I prayed with all my might that when I ripped open my presents on Christmas morning I would see that yellow box staring back at me.

I can clearly remember opening the gift that morning. I was so elated that I had gotten what I asked for. I spent hours holding that simple rectangular controller, sitting too close to the TV while leading Mario to victory.

Obviously, I'm not still filled with joy over a game that I got for Christmas over two decades ago. Natural things wear off after awhile.

However, there is a supernatural joy that comes from receiving what you've asked for in prayer. Jesus knew that. He gives us a key to attaining joy in the Holy Spirit:

> *Ask, using my name, and you will receive, and you will have abundant joy.*
> *John 16:24*

Answered prayer is a divine avenue to overwhelming joy. Before we can receive answers to our prayers, we've got to begin praying. Recent polls have shown that the average Christian prays less than five minutes a day.[3] That might seem relatively normal, but imagine what kind of a relationship you would have with your husband or wife if you only spoke to them for five minutes a day.

Quality relationships are built through communication. It's not that our culture has grown too busy to pray, we've just failed to properly prioritize our time.

When I was a youth pastor, I had students in my group that would sit in their rooms for hours playing video games. They wouldn't come out to eat, drink or shower. They were in the zone.

Adults are no different. Americans spent over five hours a day on "non-voice mobile activities," including internet use on phones and tablets in 2013.[4]

Five minutes of prayer, five hours on your iPhone. It's a perfect recipe for spiritual complacency. If you need a miracle to happen in your life, I can promise you that *Angry Birds* aren't bringing it to you.

Christian prayers have morphed into tweets to God. 140 characters verbalized for momentary satisfaction.

That's all changing.

I believe this is a generation that is latching on to the power of prayer. In the last few years we have seen a resurgence of prayer among Christians throughout North America.

Many people are choosing to begin their year with 21 days of fasting and prayer. Taking extended time to seek the face of God and cry out for our generation to be saved will never be a waste of time. Biblical prayer yields results in the natural realm and ultimately brings overwhelming joy.

THE DEVIL HATES FATHERS

The more people I talk to the more I realize that Christians don't spend more time praying because they believe they are unworthy to receive anything from God.

The enemy has worked hard to destroy the marriage relationship because he desires to skew our view of a loving father.

IF YOU DON'T KNOW HOW TO HAVE A RELATIONSHIP WITH A FATHER THAT YOU CAN SEE, HOW COULD YOU HAVE A RELATIONSHIP WITH A FATHER THAT YOU CAN'T SEE?

My heart goes out to those who grew up in broken homes, those who never knew what it was to have a father in their lives. If you were to ask many people to describe a father, they would probably say that fathers are undependable. They may say that fathers walk out and never come back.

This is exactly what the devil wants. If you don't know how to have a relationship with a father that you can see, how could you have a relationship with a Father that you can't see?

When you uncover the true nature of God for yourself, you understand what kind of a Father God is. You realize that He is not an angry, supernatural bully waiting for you to make a mistake so He can rain punishment down on you. He is a loving Father Who wants to bless and empower you with good things.

Billions of dollars are spent on Christmas presents every year and it's not just Christian parents that are buying gifts for their children. Everyone is spending money to buy presents. The Gospel of Matthew makes this kind of comparison when he writes:

> *So if you sinful people know how to give*
> *good gifts to your children, how much*
> *more will your heavenly Father give*
> *good gifts to those who ask him.*
> *Matthew 7:11*

God wants to fill our lives with His goodness. He takes great care to show us His love by showering us with the blessings of Heaven. David wrote about his experiences with God in a Psalm that says:

> *He fills my life with good things. My youth is renewed like the eagle's!*
> **Psalm 103:5**

Before you were even born, God was making plans to bless you. Your life is not an accident. You are alive because of divine design.

One of my wife's favorite scriptures is found in the book of Jeremiah. It describes the detail in which God has planned the affairs of your life:

> *"For I know the plans I have for you," says the Lord. "They are plans for good and not for disaster, to give you a future and a hope.*
> **Jeremiah 29:11**

God has a plan for every believer on the earth. Just because He has plans for our lives doesn't mean we're fulfilling them.

Life can become frustrating when we miss out on the plans of God. I outlined in a previous chapter the importance of hearing the instructions of God. When God is backing you up, things can be accomplished with ease.

If He has a plan for me, I want to know what it is!

NEVER STOP ASKING

God wants us to access His plans and thoughts through prayer. If you don't pray there is no other way to access the plans of God for your life.

The Bible is the Holy Word of God. It guides our lives in a general way. It can't tell you what college to attend or who to marry. Those decisions are accounted for in God's plan for you. He's the only one Who can tell you where your next blessing lies.

God has set people in places of authority to teach and empower us. Apostles, prophets, evangelists, pastors and teachers are ordained by God to lead the Church (Ephesians 4:11,12).

A person may speak into your life, but if God doesn't confirm in prayer what they said, don't receive it.

A minister may say that God told him I'm supposed to move to Iran and be a missionary in the Middle East, but if God didn't speak that directly to me in prayer there's no way I'm going.

Hearing from God is the only way to be sure about the future that God has prepared for your life. No one can decide it on your behalf.

One day, after my father arrived at Bible college in

Barrington, Rhode Island, he was on his way to play basketball with some friends. As he was walking through the courtyard of the college, a girl cornered him with a "word from the Lord."

"God told me you're supposed to marry me!" She exclaimed.

He stood there looking at the girl with his back against the wall, not knowing what to say. He thought, *God, if this is really You I'm converting to Buddhism!* He began to quickly ask the Lord how to respond to this girl without hurting her feelings. Suddenly, the Lord gave him the perfect answer.

"When God tells me, I'll tell you," he said and quickly ran toward the basketball court.

The Holy Spirit is available to every believer. As my father says, "God doesn't have an unlisted phone number. You can talk to Him for yourself."

God, Himself, promised to answer you when you speak to Him:

> *Ask me and I will tell you remarkable secrets you do not know about things to come.*
>
> *Jeremiah 33:3*

Prayer is the key to unlocking the mysteries of your

future. E.M. Bounds was a Methodist minister who dedicated his life to writing. Although most of his work was never published until after his death, he completed twelve manuscripts. Of the twelve books he wrote, nine were on the subject of prayer.

In one of his most famous quotes he is remembered as saying, "Much prayer, much power. Little prayer, little power. No prayer, no power."[5]

What kind of power are we talking about? It is power to accomplish your God-given purpose and make the devil cease in his harassment of your life!

Dr. David Yonggi Cho was born in 1936 to a Buddhist family in Korea. He was converted to Christianity as a young boy. God had an amazing plan for his life. After studying medicine and law, God called him to preach the gospel. Through the power of prayer God used Dr. Cho to build the largest church in the history of the world. Yoido Full Gospel Church in Seoul, Korea, has grown to over 1,000,000 members!

Understanding the vital role prayer played in the success of his ministry, Dr. Cho built "Prayer Mountain," a Christian retreat center with accommodations for 10,000 people. Prayer Mountain was built to provide a place for focused prayer and fasting for his church members and other believers.

In his book, *Prayer That Brings Revival*, Dr. Cho

writes: "There is no way we are going to see the will of God accomplished in our lives and ministry if we don't learn how to pray. Yet . . . we must first desire to pray."[6]

Your desire for the things of God will determine the level of success you see in your personal life. The Bible says:

> *Blessed are those who hunger and thirst for righteousness, For they shall be filled.*
>
> *Matthew 5:6 NKJV*

Private dedication will always lead to public reward in the kingdom of God. If we're going to walk in overwhelming joy, we have to become people who dedicate ourselves to constant prayer.

> *But you, when you pray, go into your room, and when you have shut your door, pray to your Father who is in the secret place; and your Father who sees in secret will reward you openly.*
>
> *Matthew 6:6 NKJV*

Christianity is not like other religions that dictate to their followers how many times a day they should pray, where they should be when they pray, or what they should wear while praying, but it does hint regarding the dedication of those who went before us in God's kingdom.

YOUR DEDICATION DETERMINES YOUR FINAL DESTINATION

I have had many people ask me questions like, "How long should I pray?" The short answer is, I can't tell you how long to pray. I believe that we should be led by the Holy Spirit in our prayer time.

In studying the Word of God, however, I have found some things that I feel are important in determining your routine in prayer.

When reading about Jesus and His disciples in the Gospels, and the Apostles in the book of Acts, it would seem that an hour of prayer was considered to be a standard daily routine.

- When Jesus took His disciples into the wilderness to pray He came back to find them sleeping and said, "Couldn't you watch with me even one hour? Keep watch and pray, so that you will not give in to temptation . . ." (Matthew 26:40,41)
- When Peter and John healed the lame beggar, they

were on their way to the temple at the "hour of prayer." (Acts 3:1)
- When important events were taking place sometimes Jesus prayed all through the night. (Luke 6:12)

Without a doubt, believers should engage in prayer to God on a daily basis. You wouldn't go days without talking to your husband or wife, nor should you neglect your time in the presence of God. He has things to impart to your life every single day.

Dr. Lester Sumrall was a powerful missionary statesman. He founded LeSea broadcasting and Feed the Hungry, a nonprofit organization that has delivered food and supplies to over 90 nations of the world. He saw many mighty miracles during his ministry including the documented healing of many incurable diseases.

He said that he refused to go to a business meeting, counsel those who needed help, or even take a phone call to give advice to other ministers until he had first prayed that day.

Daily prayer is a vital prerequisite for success. We see it modeled in the Bible:

- Daniel, who miraculously survived the lion's den, prayed not just once, but three times a day. (Daniel

6:10)

- When teaching His disciples how to pray, Jesus prayed, "Give us this day our daily bread . . ." Which shows us that God has things prepared for us every single day. They are received through daily prayer. (Matthew 6:11)

- As the Early Church was being formed, the Apostles realized that they had to delegate responsibilities so that they could spend their days in prayer and studying the Word of God. (Acts 6:4)

You may think that this kind of a prayer life seems daunting, but think about the time that you have available to give to the Lord.

Let's say the average American commutes fifteen minutes to work and fifteen minutes home every day. If you work forty-eight weeks a year that becomes 120 hours of driving in the car! Three entire work weeks behind the wheel. Imagine what would happen if you dedicated those driving sessions to prayer.

You will receive an infusion of supernatural joy as you pray and God answers your prayers.

KEYS TO ANSWERED PRAYER

So, according to Jesus, one of the keys to joy is not just

prayer, but having your prayers answered (John 16:24).

Some Christians feel discouraged because they pray and seemingly see no answers to their prayers. I don't blame them. That's a very disheartening place to be.

How can we ensure that our prayers are answered so that we can walk in overwhelming joy?

Does God just pick and choose which prayers to answer and which prayers to neglect? I don't believe that He does. Jesus was our prime example in every area of life. His prayers were answered continually. In fact, He said when standing before Lazarus' tomb, "Father, thank you for hearing me. You always hear me . . ." (John 11:41,42).

Therefore, there must be keys to receiving answers to prayer and walking in the momentum of Heaven's joy. Here are four checkpoints you can use in your personal prayer life.

1. Live as a child of God free from sin. Sin is a roadblock that causes God to not hear prayer (Psalm 66:18). God's ears are always open to the righteous. He always hears their prayers (1 Peter 3:12). It is the prayers of righteous men and women that produce power and bring results (James 5:16).

2. Focus your prayers on kingdom priorities. Become interested in what God is interested in. One of the

things that hinders answered prayer is selfishness (James 4:3). Selfless prayer is generated from the heart of God within you. When you seek His kingdom in that way, He has promised to add His blessing to our lives (Matthew 6:33).

3. Base your prayers on the Word of God. God can only respond to and honor His Word. He is constantly watching over His Word to perform it (Jeremiah 1:12). His Word carries an eternal strength to perform. It never returns empty (Isaiah 55:11). Find a scripture that promises what you're believing for and apply it in prayer. God has magnified His Word above His name (Psalm 138:2).

4. Always petition God in faith. Without faith you cannot please Him (Hebrews 11:6). Doubt and unbelief will short circuit the power of God in prayer (Mark 6:5,6). Any impossible situation becomes possible when faith in God is activated (Mark 9:23).

Begin petitioning God in prayer today with renewed faith and watch as things begin to change for the better. Expect answered prayer to come as you seek the face of God. Your joy will be full as you hold your testimonies in your hand!

....

"Your soul can be your best friend, empowering you to do what is right, or your worst enemy, constantly hurting your life."

....

CHAPTER SIX

GET OUT OF MY FACE

....

"For the Lord is the Spirit, and wherever
the Spirit of the Lord is, there is freedom."
—2 CORINTHIANS 3:17

Before I traveled as an evangelist, I was a youth pastor
for seven years. I still speak at youth camps and other
events that are designed for students. One question that
I have heard many times goes something like this:

"Pastor Ted, I love the Lord and I really want to stay pure
until marriage, but it's so hard in my generation! What can I
do to stay strong?"

I never give the standard youth pastor answers like,
"You just need to read your Bible more," or "Be more
faithful to your church / youth group." I always ask
them one specific question in return.

"Can I see your iPod or phone? I want to see what
music you're listening to." Usually they either reluctantly hand it over, or quickly find a reason to leave.

I discovered a pattern. The ones that were always battling these temptations were listening to the same music, filling their mind and atmosphere with the very thoughts they wanted to reject!

It's pretty hard to stay pure with your girlfriend or boyfriend when every song you listen to contains some variation of, *"girl / boy come over to my house and take off all of your clothes."*

Just doesn't work.

You might think that seems like a very trivial concept and not all that spiritual; but music is a powerful tool that can completely alter your life.

The Word of God tells the story of a king named Saul who was constantly battling depression and fear. An evil spirit would come and torment his mind on a daily basis.

His servants advised him that they knew someone who would play the harp for him. They promised that when he played, the king would be well.

He authorized them to go and find that man and bring him to the castle to play. They brought back the Psalmist David and he stayed in the king's court.

> *And whenever the tormenting spirit from God troubled Saul, David would play the harp. Then Saul would feel better, and*

the tormenting spirit would go away.
                                    1 Samuel 16:23

David never had to pray for Saul. He never even took authority over the evil spirit that troubled him. All he did was play skillfully on his harp and that evil spirit, which had brought depression, anxiety and fear, had to leave.

CONTROL YOUR ATMOSPHERE
CONTROL YOUR SOUL

When you gain control of your atmosphere and your soul, you will always win the battle against depression and anxiety.

To understand this process you must first understand that every person is made up of three very distinct parts.

. . . may your whole SPIRIT and SOUL
and BODY be kept blameless until our
Lord Jesus Christ comes again.
                                1 Thessalonians 5:23

Your Spirit is your eternal being. This is the part of you that will live eternally in either Heaven or Hell.

Once you become a Christian this part of you always wants to obey the voice and Word of God. (Romans 7:15)

Your Body is what you see in the mirror. It is the natural part of you that is growing older and slowly decaying, no matter how much make up, perfume, cologne or Axe Body Spray you use.

No matter how long you are a Christian, your natural body will always want to sin in some way. The Bible says that your body (flesh) will constantly be at war with your spirit (Galatians 5:17).

So how in the world are we supposed to be victorious with this system in place? It is the final part of you that makes the difference.

Your Soul is made up of your mind, your will and your emotions. This is the part of you that you can change for the better. Your soul can be your best friend, empowering you to do what is right, or your worst enemy, constantly harassing your life. The Bible says that a person becomes what they imagine in their heart (Proverbs 23:7).

Nothing happens by accident. Your future will never be the result of random factors. Where you arrive is always the result of a four-step process according to the Word of God.

THOUGHTS > WORDS > ACTIONS > REWARDS

The process of controlling your atmosphere begins by what you have already deposited into your own soul.

I believe with all of my heart that it is your soul that governs the well-being of your life.

Obviously, your spirit doesn't govern your life. If it did every Christian would succeed automatically and there would be no need to fight the good fight of faith.

Your body can't do anything without being given instructions from your mind. Therefore, your soul governs the well-being of your entire life.

> *Beloved, I pray that in all respects you may prosper and be in good health, JUST AS YOUR SOUL PROSPERS.*
>
> *3 John 1:2*

Interestingly, the Greek word used here for soul does not actually mean spirit. It is the Greek word *psyche* meaning our feelings, desires, affections, and aversions.

Think about it. We already know this principle to be true. If this system did not work, no company would spend tens of millions of dollars on commercial advertising.

But in fact, corporations are fighting and bidding over prime-time advertising spots so that during your favorite television program they can show you images of flame-broiled hamburgers, delicious pizza, hot french fries, and cold, chocolate milkshakes to wash it all down. Taco Bell has even coined the phrase, *"the Fourth Meal,"* encouraging people to satisfy their late-night cravings in the Taco Bell drive-through.

Advertising works.

What happens? The result is the imagery of that food is deposited into your mind. The images you see in your mind's eye create desires and cravings. The next thing you know, you've eaten two frozen pizzas before you even realize what happened.

THANKS A LOT, MORGAN!

I am a huge fan of McDonald's. I know, every health-conscious reader just had to resist the urge to shut this book, but I can't help it. To me it's delicious. So you can imagine my excitement when I found out that a movie was being released that was based on my favorite fast-food chain.

In 2004, Morgan Spurlock created the documentary *Super Size Me*. Obviously, I was slightly disappointed to find out it was a negative spin on the fast food indus-try's influence and how it encourages poor nutrition for it's own profit, but I rented it anyway.

I got home and popped the DVD into my machine

and sat back to watch Spurlock embark on a thirty-day journey in which he only ate McDonald's food for breakfast, lunch and dinner. (A glorious journey.)

Even though the movie was condemning fast-food companies for the epidemic of obesity in the United States, and the point of the film was to discourage indulging in unhealthy food, something happened to me while watching the DVD—I got hungry for McDonald's.

I couldn't help it! I was watching this guy eat all of my favorite things. The images overtook me and I had to act.

I paused the DVD about halfway through the film, jumped in my car and drove, probably faster than I should have, to the closest McDonald's.

I ordered my favorite: a double filet of fish value meal, a double cheeseburger, and so that I could be a little bit healthy, a Diet Coke, and sped back home.

I finished that documentary that was condemning McDonald's value meals—while eating a McDonald's value meal!

That's the power of your mind. It sets your life on the course that you provide, guided by the fuel with which you fill it.

It is in the thought process that actions are birthed. Ralph Waldo Emerson, the renowned American poet, once said, "The ancestor of every action is a thought." The book of Proverbs, however, says it perfectly:

> *Watch over your heart with all diligence, For from it flow the springs of life. Put away from you a deceitful mouth And put devious speech far from you.*
> **Proverbs 4:23, 24 NASB**

Isn't it interesting that after a warning against guarding your heart, which in reality is your soul, the writer instantly transitions to talking about your words? That's because your words come directly from what's inside your heart and what you've been feeding your soul.

When we meet people for the first time we often connect with them through the things that we have in common.

We talk about movies or TV shows that we like. We discuss sports and restaurants and anything that excites us. Why are we talking about those things? It is because we like them. We do them. They excite or inspire us.

Think about a man or a woman outfitted from head to toe in their favorite sports team's gear. If you ask them about the team, can you imagine them saying, "Yeah, they're okay. I'm really not that big of a fan." No way!

Do you know why? It is because no one would go to

that length to support something that they don't constantly think about and enjoy.

If you are constantly thinking about it, you will eventually talk about it. The Bible says,

> *A good person produces good things from the treasury of a good heart, and an evil person produces evil things from the treasury of an evil heart. What you say flows from what is in your heart.*
>
> *Luke 6:45*

Not only should you guard your mind, you should allow the Spirit of God to renew the spirit of your mind (Romans 12:2).

There are two main ways the Spirit will renew your mind. The first is by reading the Bible on a daily basis. The Word of God is a supernatural cleaning agent. It has the ability to wash and regenerate your mind. Look how the Apostle Paul describes it in his letter to the Ephesians:

> *[Christ] gave up his life for [the Church] to make her holy and clean, washed by the cleansing of God's word.*
>
> *Ephesians 5:25, 26*

Secondly, your mind and heart are renewed through prayer, praise and a purposeful resetting of your own thoughts. These elements work together and function as a singular tool that will bring about freedom in your atmosphere. These God-given supplements allow us to remove our focus from the elements of life that burden our minds and magnify the truth and power of God's promises.

> *Don't worry about anything; instead, pray about everything. Tell God what you need, and thank him for all he has done. Then you will experience God's peace, which exceeds anything we can understand. His peace will guard your hearts and minds as you live in Christ Jesus. And now, dear brothers and sisters, one final thing. Fix your thoughts on what is true, and honorable, and right, and pure, and lovely, and admirable. Think about things that are excellent and worthy of praise.*
>
> *Philippians 4:6-8*

By guarding and renewing your mind you will not be harassed by the spirit of this world which carries a certain heaviness that is not designed for the children of God (Isaiah 61:3).

NO NEWS IS GOOD NEWS

In the early 1990s, a woman approached my father during one of his meetings. She asked if my father would pray for her husband. He agreed to do so if she would bring him to the services.

The woman indicated that her husband was being attacked in his mind and needed deliverance.

When she brought him to the altar he looked to be on the verge of a nervous breakdown. Wanting to get more information about the situation, my Dad asked him what he'd been doing as this attack had come on his life.

At the time this story took place, the Desert Storm conflict was in full swing and the man said that he stayed home most days and watched the war on three different TVs carrying three different networks while he drank coffee.

Well, obviously, there was no spirit attacking that man's mind. He was a product of his own choices. His atmosphere was one of crisis, tension, and uncertainty mixed with a steady stream of caffeine. No wonder he was in that condition!

I don't mind knowing what's going on in the world, but I refuse to swallow the agenda of this world's system. I refuse to live in fear based upon the assumptions of "experts" who can't give you a certain picture of the future.

There comes a time in your life when you've got to ask yourself what can be a difficult question, *Who will I choose to believe?* Will I believe what I see transpiring in the world, or will I place my faith in God's Word and trust that He will care for me completely?

•　　•　　•

I was attending Bible school in Tulsa, Oklahoma, in the fall of 2001. While sitting in class one day, I heard an announcement over the loudspeaker. There was an emergency and everyone was to report to the church sanctuary immediately.

We all filed out of class and made our way to the church. We were confused. I saw some people on their cell phones trying to get more information about what had happened.

When we reached the church, they told us that a terrorist attack had taken place. Two planes hit the Twin Towers in New York City, causing them to collapse.

We all began to pray.

Later that day, my cell phone was blowing up with messages from different people. I kept hearing everyone say that we had better fill our cars with gas in case we had to get somewhere in an emergency.

When I left the church, I drove straight to the nearest gas station to get gas for my car. I was praying the whole way, "Lord, let there be gas left for me!"

When I pulled up my heart sank. There was already a long line of cars waiting for gas. I glanced at the prices on the gas station's sign. In a time when gas in Tulsa, Oklahoma was only 98¢ per gallon, the gas station had already jacked up the price to over $5.00!

I wasn't deterred. I kept praying that there would be gas for me. Finally, my turn came and I was thanking God that there was still fuel available as I pumped all my money away into my gas tank.

I went home feeling so victorious! God had made sure there was plenty of gas for me. What a miracle!

What a dummy.

I woke up the next morning and got back in my car to go to school. I passed that same gas station, only now there was no line and the price was back to normal.

I was so mad. I told God that day that I would never again make a decision that is based upon fear.

It is impossible to live in perfect peace and joy if you are constantly ingesting every fearful report that you hear. Even if the reports you receive are factual, don't receive them if they contradict the promises of God's Word that belong to you! Faith in God gives you supernatural peace and joy even when natural odds are stacked against you.

It's in those times that you not only need to have a firm faith in God's Word, but also relationships with people who share that faith with you.

A LITTLE HELP FROM MY FRIENDS

Part of cultivating an atmosphere of joy is surrounding yourself with the proper people.

We have all heard the expression, *"birds of a feather flock together."* That's because friendships are generally based on common interests. Probably the most obvious cliché we could use as an example would be what we experienced in high school. The various cliques filled the halls and cafeteria grouped tightly together. You see the athletes at one table, the studious at another, members of the band somewhere else, and the list goes on and on.

However, as life progresses people make the mistake of choosing their friends based upon common interests that are damaging to their lives.

Many times it is the hurts of the past that unite people. Maybe they have been abused or neglected by the opposite sex and that becomes their common ground. They constantly relive their mistakes because of the atmosphere they create for themselves.

What I'm telling you is not a new concept. Even secular support groups like Alcoholics' Anonymous would never recommend that someone who has finally become sober spend their time hanging around with people that are still struggling with alcoholism. Why? It is because putting yourself in the wrong group of people can ultimately destroy your future. Consider what Paul told the Corinthian Church:

> *Don't team up with those who are unbelievers. How can righteousness be a partner with wickedness? How can light live with darkness? What harmony can there be between Christ and the devil? How can a believer be a partner with an unbeliever?*
>
> *2 Corinthians 6:14,15*

This is a very important command from the Apostle Paul to believers in Corinth. He understood the importance of surrounding yourself with people of faith.

I believe that this principle extends beyond separating ourselves from sinners. I believe there are people who call themselves believers but do not believe that the entire Word of God is meant for you to experience. Let me give you an example:

What if you or one of your loved ones were battling a life-threatening disease and you were believing God for healing? You would stand on and confess God's Word and pray for healing to come. However, there are some Christians who firmly believe and teach that it is not God's will to heal everybody, and that many times God puts sicknesses on His children purposefully as a test of their faith or to teach them to be stronger believers. Furthermore, they believe that if people experience healing today it is the devil doing the work as a deception. This is obviously a false doctrine that is not supported by the Word of God.

In this scenario, would you align yourself with these "fellow believers" who are completely opposed to what you are believing? I would hope not.

We should surround ourselves with people of faith who choose to believe God regardless of circumstances. Consider this verse:

> *As iron sharpens iron, so a friend sharpens a friend.*
>
> *Proverbs 27:17*

A true friend will sharpen you and you will be able to do the same for them. Friendship should never be one-sided. I heard a minister say something once that stuck in my spirit:

"When God wants to bless you He puts a person in your life. When the devil wants to destroy you he puts a person in your life." It's very interesting that the same method can produce very different results. Don't just be drawn to people because of natural interests, but seek out the right relationships based on spiritual principles.

Gaining control of your atmosphere is a key to walking in the overwhelming joy of the Holy Spirit. Destroy every element that could draw turmoil into your life. Whether it's music, movies, bad news or wrong relationships, make a decision today to create a pocket of joy in which to live.

Remove the distractions and enemies of joy and you will find yourself resting in the perfect peace of God. This is your opportunity to take control!

#PraiseLaughRepeat

....

"Praise allows you to shed anxiety and depression and wear joy like a brand-new suit."

....

CHAPTER SEVEN

CHANGE YOUR CLOTHES

....

"To console those who mourn in Zion,
To give them beauty for ashes,
The oil of joy for mourning,
The garment of praise for the spirit of heaviness . . ."
—ISAIAH 61:3

I have a gym membership because I like to work out at least once or twice . . . a year. Anyway, this was one of those chosen days. As I walked into the gym past the long line of treadmills, I could hear faint traces of music drifting from the headphones of the runners. Some were listening to dance music, others hard rock, while some had hip hop or R&B. That gave me an idea.

I found an open treadmill for myself and climbed on it. Grabbing my iPhone, I opened YouTube and loaded a video of dynamic preaching. I set my running speed, pressed play on my iPhone and started my workout.

Something began to happen to me as I ran. The more the preacher preached, the more I felt the anointing of the Holy Spirit which translated to supernatural energy!

I bumped the treadmill speed up a few notches trying to equalize myself.

It didn't work.

The joy of the Lord was literally bubbling up in my spirit. I felt like a tea kettle that had reached the boiling point. My thoughts started racing.

Oh no, Lord! Not here. I'm in public. People might know me here. They're going to think I'm insane.

PRAISE IS ANOTHER PRESCRIPTION FROM HEAVEN THAT WILL ERADICATE DEPRESSION AND ANXIETY IN YOUR LIFE AND BRING A STEADY STREAM OF JOY INTO YOUR ATMOSPHERE.

It dawned on me that I was embarrassed to praise the Lord in public. When I realized that, I felt convicted. I couldn't help it any longer. I jumped down off of the treadmill and began shouting and dancing right in the gym. People took off for the locker room wide-eyed and glancing over at me nervously. They probably thought the gym was under a terrorist attack.

I had to make up my mind that I would never be too dignified to praise the Lord. It's a sad day when people who are promoting an evil agenda in the world have no shame in their cause. They will parade down the streets, hold $1,000 per plate dinners, use media networks and every avenue that they can to promote their agenda.

Christians, on the other hand, have become embarrassed that they serve the Almighty God. Many Christians won't even pray over their food in public because they don't want anyone to think that they're weird.

We have to get a burning love and passion for God again and cultivate a life of praise and worship.

Praise is another prescription from Heaven that will eradicate depression and anxiety in your life and bring a steady stream of joy into your atmosphere. Let's examine a passage from the Prophet Isaiah:

> *To console those who mourn in Zion, To give them beauty for ashes, The oil of joy for mourning, THE GARMENT OF PRAISE FOR THE SPIRIT OF HEAVINESS; That they may be called trees of righteousness, The planting of the Lord, that He may be glorified.*
>
> *Isaiah 61:3 NKJV*

Something important to note about this verse is that God gives us the garment of praise *FOR* the spirit of heaviness.

This is a divine trade-off that allows you to shed heaviness by engaging in praise to God. Both spirits, heaviness and praise, are compared to literal clothing so that we may gain understanding of how the process works.

MR. ROGERS STYLE

When I was growing up there was a television show for children called *Mr. Rogers' Neighborhood*.

Every day, Mr. Rogers would enter the house dressed in a suit and tie singing the theme song, *Won't You Be My Neighbor*. As he sang, he would open his closet, hang up his suit jacket and put on a colored sweater.

There's no way that he could have put the sweater on over his suit jacket. You have to make a choice. It's either the suit jacket or the sweater.

The same is true regarding the overwhelming joy of the Holy Spirit. You can't decide you're going to keep some of your depression and anxiety but also walk in a bit of joy. It's one or the other.

Praise is a master key to accessing joy in the Spirit. Divine intervention is provoked by man's celebration. This was the determining factor for the Apostle Paul and his friend Silas after they had been beaten and locked in prison for preaching the gospel and performing miracles.

And at midnight Paul and Silas prayed,

> *and sang praises unto God: and the pris-*
> *oners heard them.*
>
> ### Acts 16:25 KJV

At midnight, in their darkest hour, when it would have been easy to be frustrated or afraid for their lives, they chose to praise God.

It wasn't some little *Kumbaya-by-the-campfire* type of praise. They weren't muttering somber hymns quietly under their breath. The Bible says that although they were locked in the inner dungeon, as they began to sing and praise God, all of the prisoners heard them! They obviously praised God loudly and fervently. I will always remember this phrase that I heard taught by Dr. David Oyedepo:

> *You will not be free from frustration until*
> *you commit to a life of celebration.*

Praise brings freedom from the attacks of the enemy. You can literally praise your way into the joy of the Lord. Look at the result of their praise that night in the dungeons:

> **And suddenly there was a great earth-**
> **quake, so that the foundations of the**

prison were shaken: and immediately all the doors were opened, and every one's bands were loosed.

Acts 16:26 KJV

Did you see what was hidden in that verse? The Bible doesn't say that only Paul and Silas experienced freedom. It says that *all* the doors were opened and *everyone's* bands were loosed!

Your praise can bring freedom to your family and your loved ones. Your children will be affected by what you choose to do today. Will you allow the spirit of heaviness to rule your home, or will you put on a garment of praise and strip off that evil spirit of heaviness?

We have to realize that praise is not limited to the times that we feel like doing it. We don't praise God only when we receive our answers, but more importantly, we praise Him before we see the end result of our prayers. That is the true essence of faith!

GET YOUR BACK UP OFF THE WALL

Smith Wigglesworth was a British evangelist from Bradford, England. He was born in 1859 to a very poor family and grew up having a hunger to do great things for God. His life was marked by amazing miracles of healing and deliverance.

During his ministry it was confirmed and documented that fourteen people were raised from the dead, one of whom was his own wife, Polly Wigglesworth.

Those who wrote about him said that one of the main characteristics that set his life apart was his dedication to praising the Lord. It was said that throughout his life he would get out of bed every morning and dance before the Lord for ten minutes thanking God for giving him another day to serve Him and live for Him.[7]

Whether you are a night person or a morning person, nobody wakes up every morning feeling like dancing. It takes a dedication to praise God like that!

You have to consciously decide that no matter what may be going on in your life, you're going to praise the Lord. This is what the Bible refers to as a "sacrifice of praise."

> *Therefore, let us offer through Jesus a continual sacrifice of praise to God, proclaiming our allegiance to his name.*
> *Hebrews 13:15*

I don't just preach this principle, I have to live it also. I can remember an Easter Sunday morning over a decade ago when I was still on staff as the worship leader at our home church. I woke up that morning as sick as I had ever been. The enemy had tried to put the flu on my body, and the symptoms were firing on all cylinders.

I hardly felt like moving that morning. Let alone getting dressed to go to church to sing, praise and usher in the presence of the Lord.

I felt the conviction of the Spirit of God. I had preached this many times before and now it was my time to activate it in my own life.

I got out of bed, showered and slowly dressed for church. When I got there I told the band and choir to just keep praising and singing no matter what happened that morning. I told them even if they saw me run off of the platform and out of the church, just keep going.

We began the service. As I sang and played, I looked out over the crowd and all I could see were white dots. I had a splitting headache and my stomach was completely nauseated. However, something began to happen as I sang and praised the Lord. My vision returned to normal, my headache left, and my stomach was settled. By the time I was done singing and praising that morning, every bit of the flu had gone out of my body and I was completely healed!

There is a reason why things like this happen. *Divine intervention is provoked by man's celebration.* The Bible is clear that praise is God's favorite atmosphere.

> *But You are holy, Enthroned in the prais-*
> *es of Israel. Our fathers trusted in You;*
> *They trusted, and You delivered them.*
> **Psalm 22:3,4 NKJV**

I have often said that if you refuse to offer praises to God, He has nothing in your atmosphere to get involved with. If He inhabits our praises, then we must construct an environment that He not only abides in, but can operate in and show Himself mighty!

People who live a life without praise are relegated to living a life without power. The power that I'm talking about is the supernatural assistance of God on your behalf.

Praising God unleashes heavenly forces to aid you in expediently accomplishing your purpose.

SEND JUDAH FIRST

Think about how insane it is to have a vast army of soldiers coming against you with the sole purpose of wiping you off the face of the earth. Most commanders would put their most skilled warriors on the front lines to reach the battle first. That makes sense.

Israel, however, understood the principle of praise. They assigned Judah, one of the twelve tribes of Israel, to be the first group on the battlefield. Except Judah didn't carry any weapons—only musical instruments!

Their assignment was to sing and praise God as they marched toward the enemy armies. As they did, God caused the enemy armies to begin fighting among themselves. They killed each other until no one was left. When Judah arrived at the lookout point in the wilderness, all they saw were dead bodies lying on the ground as far as they could see. Not a single one of their enemies had escaped! (2 Chronicles 20).

They didn't have to swing one sword or hold up one shield. God fought on their behalf. Which gives us a life-changing principle that we must embrace to access the joy and peace of Heaven:

> *Do not be afraid! Don't be discouraged . .*
> *. for the battle is not yours, but God's.*
> *2 Chronicles 20:15*

It is God's desire to fight on our behalf. That's why we are encouraged to give Him our worries and anxieties. Praise is such a powerful catalyst in God's kingdom. It's importance cannot be ignored. Neither can we afford to dismiss the discipline of praising God daily in our own lives.

Praise brings change for the better.

Maybe you're in a position where you feel like you've lost out on the goodness of God in your personal life. I want to encourage you. Your story is not over. You can get back what the enemy has stolen from you. You can recover!

RECOVERY WITHOUT REHAB

Leprosy is a terrible disease. It eats a person's flesh and the organs of their body. It was also very contagious in Jesus' day. In fact, when the Law of Moses was given it was commanded that all lepers were to live outside of town by themselves (Leviticus 13). If they were caught coming into contact with others who didn't have leprosy they were to be stoned to death.

One day, when Jesus was traveling toward Jerusalem, He came in contact with ten lepers. They began crying out to Him for mercy. He told them to go show themselves to the priests. (Which was the custom according to the Law of Moses. Only the priests could declare a person cleansed of leprosy.) As they turned to go, they were healed of the disease.

One of the ten turned around and came back to Jesus and fell to the ground, thanking and praising Him. Jesus told him to stand up and go, for his faith had "made him whole."

Let me show you the difference between what happened to this leper as opposed to the other nine. The nine were cleansed of their leprosy, but whatever body parts they had lost were still missing.

The leper who returned to give thanks, however, was not only cleansed of leprosy, but Jesus said he was *made whole.* You cannot be whole if pieces of you are missing. The fact that he returned to give Jesus praise provoked Christ to take him a step further!

THE DEVIL CANNOT DEFEAT YOU, BUT HE CAN TEMPT YOU TO DEFEAT YOURSELF BY NEGLECTING TO REJOICE IN THE LORD.

This man recovered what he had lost to leprosy by praising and thanking Jesus.

Maybe your children aren't serving the Lord or you are believing for your spouse to be saved. Possibly you have experienced a financial crisis. Is your health not where you want it to be?

Begin praising God for what He is going to do in your life. Build an atmosphere in your home that God can inhabit. Prepare yourself to see change for the better as God begins to fight on your behalf.

The devil doesn't want you to engage in praise to God because he knows what the end result will be. He cannot defeat you, but he can tempt you to defeat yourself by neglecting to rejoice in the Lord.

DON'T HANG UP YOUR HARP

The temptation is to let yourself react normally to the situation at hand. It seems normal to fall into fear when you receive a bad medical report or worry when your family seems to be off track.

Do not let your situation define your response! This was the mistake the captives made in the book of Psalms:

> *Beside the rivers of Babylon, we sat and wept as we thought of Jerusalem. WE PUT AWAY OUR HARPS, hanging them on the branches of the poplar trees.*
> *Psalm 137:1–2*

Keep your harp in hand! Whether you need a miracle or everything is going well, don't let your praise get dusty on the shelf. Your dedication will define your final destination. Let your praise unlock the door to a brand-new realm of overwhelming joy!

"Winning souls for Jesus brings an infusion of joy and strength that cannot come any other way."

CHAPTER EIGHT

SOUL MAGNET

*"Crowds listened intently to Philip . . . And many
who had been paralyzed or lame were healed.
So there was great joy in that city."*
— ACTS 8:6,8

I stood on the platform of my old high school auditorium. I was asked to come back and speak in the Bible club that was held once a month. I looked across the crowd that day. There were a few hundred students in attendance.

I knew not everyone was there because they were excited about the Bible. In fact, most of them were probably coming so they could get a free period out of their classes.

It didn't matter to me. I had just graduated from Bible school and I was on fire and excited to do great things for God.

I can still remember what I preached that day: *"Don't Make God Vomit."* I took my reference from Revelation

3:16. I spoke about the fact that God would rather you be an on fire Christian or a cold sinner. Anything in between makes Him sick. I gave it everything I had. I knew from experience that there were plenty of people who claimed to be Christians but they hadn't fully dedicated themselves to Jesus Christ.

As I neared the end of my message I gave the students an opportunity to make a personal decision to give their lives to Jesus.

"If you know there is something in your life that is holding you back from serving God, today is your day to make a change," I said.

As their heads were bowed and their eyes closed I gave the invitation for salvation. I encouraged them to come to the front to pray with me.

Crickets.

No one moved. I was embarrassed. I felt like a failure. I preached my guts out and not one person responded to the altar call. I was like the antithesis of Billy Graham.

My first instinct was to quickly close the service in prayer and get out of there in a hurry. Right before I did, the Holy Spirit prompted me to wait.

I stood there feeling stupid. My mind was racing back over all of the things I could have said or done differently during the service.

All of a sudden, a girl got up out of her seat and started walking to the front of the auditorium. Honestly, she looked like the last person that would have responded to an altar call. She looked like a Hot Topic model. She was clad in dark, gothic makeup, black clothes and black nail polish. I saw that she was crying as she made her way forward.

The Holy Spirit was calling her to Jesus.

If she had been the only person that answered the altar call that day, I would have been happy. However, something began to happen. After she came to the altar other students began to get out of their seats and come also. One by one, they filtered from the theater seats, down the aisles and grouped around the stage.

Well over one hundred students gave their hearts to Jesus that day in a public high school. I was so happy to see God working in their lives.

It was that day that I realized that there is overwhelming joy connected with soul-winning and demonstrating the power of God.

CITYWIDE JOY

We must become less focused on ourselves and more focused on those God has called us to reach. In the United States of America there is a temptation to live a very selfish Christianity.

It's easy to constantly focus on yourself, but in doing so you miss the bigger picture of the people who are in your circle of influence.

I'm not against believers walking in their divine blessing. On the contrary, if you are not blessed you don't have the ability to bless someone else.

However, when you activate your purpose and begin to touch people around you with the gospel of Christ, you will receive an infusion of joy and strength that cannot come any other way.

That is what happened to Philip. According to Acts chapter 8, the believers had been receiving persecution in Jerusalem and as a result they were scattered through the regions of Judea and Samaria.

Philip found himself in Samaria and began to preach to the Samarians. Crowds began to gather to hear him preach and see him perform miracles in the name of Jesus.

Look at the result of his efforts:

> *Many evil spirits were cast out, screaming as they left their victims. And many who had been paralyzed or lame were healed. So THERE WAS GREAT JOY IN THAT CITY.*
>
> *Acts 8:7,8*

Citywide joy was the result of one man's soul-winning and miracle ministry! It didn't take a massive team of people. It took one man who decided that he was going to bring the power of Jesus Christ to the forefront.

Imagine what you could accomplish for God in your city or town! You might be thinking that there is no way you could ever stand on a platform and preach to people. Maybe you feel like you are too shy or awkward to approach people with the gospel.

The good news is God has given everyone individual gifts and He uses us all differently. The power of the Holy Spirit is the boldness you need to activate your gifts and talents for the Lord.

CHOCOLATE CAKE EVANGELISM

There was a woman who attended a church in Chicago who was gifted to bake cakes, pies and cookies. I don't mean Betty Crocker style; I'm talking everything made from scratch.

One morning she woke up and the Holy Spirit prompted her to go downstairs and bake a chocolate cake.

"Lord, you know I don't even like chocolate cake," she responded aloud. However, following the leading of the Spirit she went downstairs and got busy baking.

When her oven timer beeped, she pulled out a fresh, delicious chocolate cake. When it was ready to eat, the Lord spoke to her again and said,

"Take that chocolate cake to the lady who lives next door and give it to her."

Obediently, she wrapped up the cake, put on her shoes and went next door. She rang the doorbell, and when her neighbor opened it she handed her the chocolate cake and told her she had baked it just for her.

"You did?" Her neighbor exclaimed. "I just told my husband yesterday that I could go for a good piece of chocolate cake!"

Her neighbor invited her in the house and they sat at the kitchen table enjoying chocolate cake and hot tea together.

As they were talking, she led her neighbor to Jesus!

When she woke up the next morning, the Holy Spirit spoke to her again and told her to bake another chocolate cake. This time she didn't argue. She knew what was happening.

She repeated the process of baking the chocolate cake the same as the previous day. When it was ready she felt impressed by God to go three doors down and give the cake to the woman who lived in that house.

The result was the same! She won that lady to Jesus over chocolate cake at the table.

By the time it was all said and done, her pastor testified that she had filled three rows of their church with people for whom she had baked chocolate cakes!

She never had to stand on one platform or hold one microphone. God anointed her to fulfill the Great Commission simply by doing what she was gifted to do.

Examine your life today. What has God entrusted you with? What are your gifts and talents? Have you given them to God so that He can use you to bring in a harvest of souls?

Don't let anything stand in your way of bringing your friends and loved ones to Heaven with you. Jesus is coming back very soon and there is a mission to be accomplished.

SOUL GOALS

I'm sure you know at least ten people who are not serving Jesus Christ—people who you have a relationship with and talk to on a regular basis.

This is your starting point. Write down their names, pray for them and ultimately show them the love of Christ and bring them to Jesus.

My uncle, Evangelist Tiff Shuttlesworth, once said, "It's hard to hit a target you can't see, but it's impossible to hit a target you don't have."

Set goals for your soul-winning life and ask God to empower you to accomplish them. As you pray, ask God to give you supernatural opportunities and open doors into the lives of those for whom you're praying.

It's important that we recognize supernatural opportunities when they are presented to us by the Holy Spirit.

IT'S HARD TO HIT A TARGET YOU CAN'T SEE, BUT IT'S IMPOSSIBLE TO HIT A TARGET YOU DON'T HAVE.

It will be no accident when people begin to ask your opinion about the end of the world or what you think happens when you die. These are moments in which God is opening a door for you to minister the gospel of Jesus Christ to someone in need.

Paul encouraged the Church in Ephesus:

> *So be careful how you live. Don't live like fools, but like those who are wise. Make the most of every opportunity in these evil days.*
>
> *Ephesians 5:15,16*

Charles Spurgeon, arguably the greatest preacher of the 19th Century, once said, "To be a soul winner is the happiest thing in the world. And with every soul you bring to Jesus Christ, you seem to get a new heaven here upon earth."

I had the privilege of meeting Dr. Reinhard Bonnke, who is possibly the most effective evangelist in the history of the Christian Church. His ministry has seen over 42 million documented salvations in the last five years as of 2014.[8]

This is a man who has preached to a crowd of over 1.6 million individuals in a single meeting and seen over one million people respond to the salvation altar call in a single service!

If you don't know who he is, I encourage you to Google him and look at the pictures of some of his overseas crusades. What he has done for the kingdom of God is truly amazing.

He led us into his office in Orlando, Florida, and said, "I want to show you something." He explained that a composer who scores films created a promotional video using clips of his altar calls.

We sat down on the couch as he put in the DVD and pressed play. I remember tears streaming down my face as I watched millions of people responding to the mighty gospel of Jesus Christ.

I saw the service in Africa where 1.03 million people came forward to receive Jesus as their savior in one night.

I could feel the joy of the Holy Spirit as I witnessed multitudes of people being converted to Christ.

There is not only an overwhelming joy that comes from winning people to the Lord as Jesus commanded, but a fulfillment that cannot come any other way.

CHRISTIANITY IS NOT A DEAD HISTORY. IT IS A LIVING ORGANISM THAT IS STILL PRODUCING RESULTS TODAY.

It is time for us to decide that we must see God change our generation. I'm thankful for what He did for my grandparents and my parents. I love to hear the testimonies through the ages, but Christianity is not a dead history. It is a living organism that is still producing results today.

We are part of the only religion that cannot take you to the grave where the founder's bones can be found. Jesus is alive and He is coming back very soon.

As you begin to activate your gift and win souls, you will find yourself walking in a joy and fulfillment that is unspeakable! All we have to do is lift up Jesus. He said:

> *And when I am lifted up from the earth, I will draw everyone to myself.*
>
> *John 12:32*

I'm sure Charles Spurgeon made more than a few

people angry when he said, "Every Christian is either a missionary or an imposter."

Our time is now. Let's declare together, "I refuse to let my friends and family to go to hell! My generation will be saved!"

"*Dedicated givers aren't only qualified for a financial harvest, but also a harvest of supernatural joy.*"

CHAPTER NINE

PARADOX CITY

···

"It is more blessed (makes one happier and
more to be envied) to give than to receive."
— ACTS 20:35

"We're so happy we closed on our new house!"

"I just got a new car! I love it, I'm so glad I was able to get it." These are phrases we hear constantly and are common among Americans. We have been conditioned to believe that if we could only acquire the next new thing, we would be happy. After all, who could possibly be happy with last year's model (insert thing here)?

We are being marketed to daily. TV commercials, radio spots, internet banners and spam e-mails promise us success and joy for the low price of . . . you get the picture.

If that isn't enough, they always show us pictures of the happiest, skinniest, tannest, people with the whitest teeth you've ever seen enjoying their product.

The problem is, there isn't a product available that can bring you joy. It turns out keeping up with the Joneses can take a harsh toll on your psychological well-being.

A new study from the San Francisco Federal Reserve concludes that suicide is more common in rich neighborhoods.[9] The lack of contentment in the lives of Americans has driven them to destruction.

Let me state very clearly that I am in no way opposed to the blessing of the Lord. I have not and will never take a vow of poverty. It is not God's plan for any believer to be poor or lack in any area (2 Corinthians 8:9).

The key is receiving supernatural contentment in your life. The Apostle Paul said:

> *. . . for I have learned how to be content (satisfied to the point where I am not disturbed or disquieted) in whatever state I am.*
>
> *Philippians 4:11 AMP*

Letting go of the desire for natural things and developing a God-given hunger for heavenly things will bring you freedom to access overwhelming joy.

Remember that it is God Who is responsible for every blessing in your life. Any increase or promotion that you will experience is a direct result of God bringing it into your possession (Psalm 75:6,7 AMP).

God said that we should have no other gods before Him (Exodus 20:3). The Bible says that God is "jealous" (Deuteronomy 6:15). This simply means that He wants all of your worship and love. When something in your life is placed at a higher priority level than God, it becomes an idol and a hazard to your spiritual success.

Why would God release something into your life that He knows will take you further from Him? He won't.

In fact, you'll find that when you stop caring about the things of this world, God will allow you to become a steward of them. This is because He knows that if He commanded you to give it away, you're not so tied to your possessions that you would hesitate.

Giving is a primary path to living in overwhelming joy in the Holy Spirit.

Many people never catch on to the paradox of God's economic system. If you want to experience increase, you must give what you have. God said He would supernaturally cause people to seek you out and pour into your life (Luke 6:38).

Logical thinking would say that if you want to have more money you should do less giving and more saving. Take the finances that you would normally sow into the kingdom of God and begin to put them in an interest-bearing account. Actually, the opposite is true according to the Word of God. The writer of Proverbs said:

> *There is one who scatters, yet increases more; and there is one who withholds more than is right, but it leads to poverty.*
>
> *Proverbs 11:24 NKJV*

When the Holy Spirit speaks to our hearts giving instruction regarding what we should sow financially; He is presenting an opportunity not only for financial increase, but also for joy!

GIVE. LAUGH. REPEAT.

Once, when I was praying and studying this subject, the Holy Spirit directed me to the story of the rich young ruler found in Matthew chapter 19.

A wealthy, influential man approached Jesus with the desire to have eternal life. He asked Jesus what good deed he had to do to have it. Jesus simply told him that if he wanted to receive eternal life, he had to keep the commandments.

"I've done that since I was a young boy. Is there anything else I must do?" The young ruler replied.

Jesus proceeded to give him a very specific instruction. "Go and sell all your possessions and give the money to the poor, and you will have treasure in Heaven. Then come, follow me."

The story ends by saying, "when the young man heard this, he went away sad, for he had many possessions (Matthew 19:16-22).

When I read that, the Lord impressed my spirit with this thought: *"Not only did this young man miss out on receiving a financial harvest when he chose not to give what Jesus commanded him, he also opened the door and dismissed joy from his life."*

Here is the question. How many other people did Jesus instruct to give away all of their possessions before they came to follow Him?

None.

Jesus apparently realized by the Spirit that this man had an issue with the riches in his life. My grandfather, A.E. Shuttlesworth used to say, "The Bible says that he had many possessions, but in reality, many possessions had him."

He went away sad.

When we obey the instructions of God regarding our life of giving, the joy of Heaven will flood our lives.

One scripture that is extremely important to see as we discuss the joy that is activated by our giving is found in the book of Acts when the Apostle Paul quotes the words of Jesus Christ:

> *It is more blessed (makes one happier and more to be envied) to give than to receive.*
>
> *Acts 20:35 AMP*

Giving places you on a higher plane. Think about it, anyone can receive something, but not everyone has the ability to give.

BUDDY BARREL

It is so important to teach our children the joy of giving at an early age. Embedding spiritual principles in their hearts will form heavenly habits that promise to yield results throughout their entire lives.

In his classic book, *Rich Dad, Poor Dad*, Robert Kiyosaki teaches principles that show us why the rich stay rich and the poor stay poor. Year after year it remains the same. The percentage of families that acquire "new wealth" is small compared to those that maintain the wealth they already have.

According to Kiyosaki, it is because wealth and success are not about the resources in your possession, rather, the system of disciplines by which you abide.[10]

This thought is mirrored in the Word of God. The writer of Proverbs is clear that when you train your children to live according to Biblical principles they will continue in them as they grow older (Proverbs 22:6).

When I was a young boy, my family attended Calvary Temple Assembly of God church in Worthington, West Virginia, which was pastored by my grandfather.

The Assemblies of God denomination had developed an initiative called BGMC to teach children the importance of giving toward overseas missions. They even came up with a cartoon mascot to represent the program. His name was Buddy Barrel.

When BGMC started in 1949, supplies were shipped by boat to the missionaries in barrels. Barrels were used because they could be sealed tight and made waterproof. This way the supplies would not get wet or ruined. As a result Buddy Barrel was created.

In short, Buddy Barrel was basically a piggy bank for your missions giving. It was a small, plastic, yellow barrel with an orange cap that had a slot you could drop your coins into.

Every month, our children's church class was encouraged to fill our Buddy Barrels with as much change as we could lay our hands on. Many times we held friendly competitions to see whether the boys or the girls would give the higher monthly total.

Needless to say, I had to constantly resist the urge to dive into the koi pond at the local Chinese restaurant and rob them of all the change under the water. (At seven years old I had the makings of a bank robber.)

Not to mention, the rowdy boys of our church developed a trend, we all loved to make our Buddy Barrels as heavy as possible so that we could engage in our other favorite Missions Sunday past time — throwing the barrels at each other's heads.

We were being taught at a young age how to experience the joy of giving. Over twenty-five years have passed, and although I am no longer on speaking terms with Buddy Barrel, the love for giving to God that was developed in me at an early age has only grown stronger through the years. There is nothing like becoming a blessing to someone else!

As children of Abraham, we are part of a holy lineage in which God promised that He would bless us and make us a blessing! (Genesis 12:2).

In order to be a blessing to someone else, you must first be blessed. You cannot give what you don't have. That means that God's promise to us through Abraham literally positions us to be an eternal blessing to the people of the earth!

There is no joy in giving if you are pressured or manipulated into doing it. That's because God never designed your giving to be laborious, on the contrary it is a part of your worship toward Him. That's why the Apostle Paul encouraged the Corinthian Church:

You must each decide in your heart how much to give. And don't give reluctantly or in response to pressure. "For God loves a person who gives cheerfully."
2 Corinthians 9:7

Manipulation takes the joy out of giving. Our decisions in giving should always be directed by the instructions we receive from the Holy Spirit. When God speaks to you to give, He has a harvest ready to send back.

THE BIGGEST OFFERING IN HISTORY

King David was coming to a transitional period in his reign over Israel. His son Solomon had been chosen to become the next king and was tasked with building the temple of God.

David gathered gold, silver, bronze, iron, wood, onyx, other precious stones, costly jewels, and all kinds of fine stone and marble for the building project. (Needless to say they didn't require the hand-drawn thermometer on white poster board that gets colored in when people give that I've seen in many churches.)

If that wasn't enough, he decided to give all of his own private treasures to assist in the building of the temple. David gave 112 tons of gold and 262 tons of refined silver.

In today's market, David's giving is valued at over $5.5 billion! When all of the other leaders saw what David was giving they gave 188 tons of gold, 375 tons of silver, 675 tons of bronze, as well as many precious stones!

The total amount of wealth given to build God's temple that day is valued at over $20 billion! (1 Chronicles 29:1-8).

To put that in perspective, Yankee Stadium cost $1.5 billion to build.[11] You could build thirteen Yankee Stadiums for the cost of God's temple in King David's day and still have $500 million left over!

Look what the Bible says happened after they all gave their offerings:

> *The people rejoiced over the offerings, for they had given freely and wholeheartedly to the Lord, and King David was filled with joy.*
>
> *1 Chronicles 29:9*

Interestingly, people who don't understand the joy that accompanies freely giving to God always assume that when you give away something of value it always hurts. On the contrary, when you obey the instructions of the Spirit of God and give what He speaks to you, overwhelming joy will flood your soul!

David was *completely filled* with joy after he gave all of his own private treasures to build the house of God.

There is no question about it, giving brings a joy to your spirit that nothing else can bring.

Notice that the joy didn't come as a result of the harvest they received for their giving, although there is a great joy in receiving your harvest (Psalm 126:5,6). They rejoiced at the moment of release! The simple act of giving instantly activated the joy of God's Spirit in their hearts.

Those who dedicate themselves to consistently sow exempt themselves from having to suffer stagnation.

Determine in your heart that not only will you set giving goals this year, but you will follow through with consistency and laugh as your seed leaves your hand.

#PraiseLaughRepeat

....

"When God makes the impossible possible, all you can do is laugh and rejoice."

....

CHAPTER TEN

DIVINE INTERRUPTION
·······································
"We were filled with laughter, and we sang for joy.
And the other nations said, "What amazing things
the Lord has done for them.""
—PSALM 126:2

One summer, when I was still attending high school in West Virginia, I was swimming in our pool when the phone rang. It was a friend of mine calling from the hospital with bad news.

Another one of my friends was returning from a party the night before when the driver of the car he was riding in swerved off the road and crashed.

When the accident took place my friend was struck in the temple and it put him into a coma. That morning he was lying in a hospital bed with brain trauma and the doctors said it didn't look good.

My friend asked me over the phone if I would come to the hospital and pray for him.

I dried off, got dressed and called someone to come

123

pick me up since I didn't have my license yet.

When we arrived at the hospital there was already a group of students from my school in the waiting area. It was a very somber atmosphere. A few students were crying. It was a serious situation.

I was told that his brain trauma had been severe and even if he did wake up from the coma, he may have sustained loss of memory, motor skills and other side effects.

I walked to the other side of the waiting room and began to pray in the Holy Spirit. Interestingly, the more I prayed, the more angry I became. I wasn't mad in the natural, it was a righteous indignation that arose within me. I was mad at the devil for trying to kill my friend.

I paced back and forth, praying fervently that the power of God would touch my friend. I could feel my faith being stimulated as I prayed in the Holy Spirit (Jude 1:20).

Finally, I got to the point where praying wasn't enough and I began walking briskly toward the intensive care unit.

Nurses tried to stop me and told me that only immediate family members were allowed in his room. I refused to be deterred. I think they may have seen the boldness in my eyes and just let me go.

I was on a mission.

When I walked into his room I found him lying on the hospital bed with his body connected to multiple machines.

His mother, a wonderful woman, was sitting in a chair in the corner of the room. With tears in her eyes, she thanked me for coming. What a horrible thing to have to see your child suffer.

I knelt down next to him and with my mouth close to his ear I said, "I don't know if you can hear me, but it's Ted. I came to get you out of here."

I laid my hands on his lifeless body and asked the Holy Spirit to heal him. I prayed that not only would he regain consciousness, but he would have no memory loss, weakness or loss of his motor skills.

When I finished praying I stood up and told his mother everything was going to be okay. He looked no different. He was still in the coma. He didn't instantly wake up and run around the hospital. However, the fact that I didn't instantly see the manifestation of my prayer didn't weaken my faith. I understood that you don't be-lieve that it's a finished work when you *see it happen*, you believe it's finished *when you pray!* (Mark 11:24).

I went home and got back in the pool. The very next day I received another call from a friend at the hospital.

His voice was charged with energy. "Ted, you're nev-er going to believe what happened."

"What happened?" I asked.

"He came out of the coma!" My friend exclaimed. "Plus, he has no memory loss, no damage to his motor skills and the nurses say that they have never seen anyone recover this quickly or thoroughly from serious brain trauma!"

When I heard that I began to rejoice in the spirit. When God interrupts the natural order of life and performs mighty miracles, it brings overwhelming joy into your life! The miracle power of God is proof that Jesus is still alive today!

Miracles are another important path to walking in overflowing joy on a daily basis. Miracles shouldn't be scarce in the life of a believer. They should be natural.

When God steps in and makes an impossible situation possible, it is cause for immediate rejoicing!

> *When the Lord brought back his exiles to Jerusalem, it was like a dream! We were filled with laughter, and we sang for joy. And the other [heathen] nations said, "What amazing things the Lord has done for them."*
>
> *Psalm 126:1,2*

One of my favorite elements of this passage is the fact

that God performed such mighty miracles among His people that even those who didn't serve Him had to declare that He was moving on behalf of His children!

God's goodness is designed to draw people to Jesus (Romans 2:4).

Unfortunately, not everyone believes God's miracles are for today. Cessationism is the erroneous belief that the signs, wonders and miracles that God performed in His Word ceased when the last original apostle died. Not only is that untrue, this belief system cuts you off from walking in this avenue of supernatural joy!

Everything you receive comes through faith. Simply put, if you don't believe it, you cannot receive it. One of my favorite scriptures is found in the Gospel of Mark as Jesus encourages a father who is weak in faith:

> *If you can believe, all things are possible to him who believes.*
>
> ### Mark 9:23 NKJV

Faith is required to receive the miracles of Heaven in your life. Jesus said that we must learn to receive the kingdom of God like a child (Mark 10:15).

How does a child receive something? They believe what they're told. They haven't developed a distrust for people that makes them question what they hear.

Faith doesn't put the Word of God through the filter of the facts and opinions of the natural world.

I've heard people make statements like, "I know God is a healer, but cancer is a serious thing that many people don't survive."

So what are they saying? Is their case somehow special? Does God's eternal power not extend to their specific type of illness?

That type of thinking is a ploy of the devil to make you believe that you are disqualified from receiving God's power in your own personal life.

God wants you to see Him through eyes of faith knowing that He can accomplish anything on your behalf. Once, when speaking to the prophet Jeremiah, He said:

> *"I am the Lord, the God of all the peoples of the world. Is anything too hard for me?"*
>
> *Jeremiah 32:27*

God has a specific desire to show Himself mighty on behalf of His children. He is constantly seeking someone to whom He can show His mighty power (2 Chronicles 16:9). I pray that you will be the person who receives the magnificent blessings of Heaven today.

The power of God in action always brings rejoicing!

THE JOY OF DEMONSTRATION

In Acts chapter 3, Peter and John were on their way to the temple to pray when they encountered a lame man begging for money at the gate.

They encouraged him by offering something to help him — they began to demonstrate the power of the Spirit as they instructed him to rise up and walk. Apparently, he wasn't moving fast enough for them because Peter reached down, grabbed him and pulled him to his feet. The story finishes:

> *He jumped up, stood on his feet, and began to walk! Then, walking, leaping, and praising God, he went into the Temple with them. All the people saw him walking and heard him praising God.*
>
> *Acts 3:8,9*

The demonstration of God's miracle power brought instantaneous joy!

Not long ago, I was holding a revival meeting outside of Charlotte, North Carolina. One night as I was ministering the Lord prompted me to pray for an elderly woman in the crowd. The Holy Spirit spoke to me that she was going deaf and needed to receive healing.

She came forward and I could feel her strong faith to receive a miracle.

"Do you believe that when I pray for you God will open your ears?" I asked.

"Oh, I know He will!" She exclaimed.

I laid my hands on her and commanded her to be healed. When I removed my hand and finished praying, that elderly woman began to hop and dance across the altar as her hearing came back instantly.

Everyone could hear her as she shouted, "Thank you, Jesus! I knew You would! I knew You would!"

Something wonderful happens when God connects with your faith in Him and interrupts your situation by imparting His glory. You gain access to an advance preview of Heaven's atmosphere!

"Enter into the joy of the Lord."

This is the phrase the Bible uses in the Gospel of Matthew to describe entering into Heaven's glory (Matthew 25:21). We are walking directly into the joy of the Lord.

God never intended for you to have to wait until Heaven to experience His overwhelming joy. In order to impart a sneak preview of His wonder, God gave us the ability to experience His power through miracles.

In Genesis, we read the story of Abraham and Sarah.

God promised Abraham that he would be the father of many nations. Abraham hadn't even had a child.

How was he to be the father of many nations when he hadn't even had a son of his own? In fact, they had reached the late stages of life and considered themselves too old to have children. Abraham was one hundred years old and Sarah was ninety-one!

It would be impossible for them to have a child at that age . . . in the natural. When God is involved, however, He makes the natural supernatural!

Not only did God promise Sarah that she would have a son, she gave birth to him exactly when God said that she would.

When Isaac was born she made a very interesting comment:

> **And Sarah declared, "God has brought me laughter. All who hear about this will laugh with me."**
>
> **Genesis 21:6**

When she received the miracle that God promised, it caused her to receive supernatural laughter. Not only that, but those who would experience the testimony of God's power in her life would also laugh with her.

Miracles contain such dynamic power that they encourage not only those who receive, but even those who hear the testimony of them.

MADELYN'S MIRACLE

Carolyn and I have experienced the joy of God's power in our own life and family. At the end of 2012 as I finished our first tent meeting, the enemy attacked my young daughter, Madelyn.

We didn't understand why our daughter, who was normally so full of energy and life, was so lethargic. She had lost all energy and even stopped walking and had to be carried everywhere.

When we got home we took her to the doctor to find out what was going on. The doctor sat us down and told us that Madelyn had a very rare blood disease that was affecting her body. They told us that she would have to be on medication and have routine heart check ups for the rest of her life.

The enemy attacked my mind.

Not only did he try to tell me that my daughter wasn't going to survive, he made me feel as though I had no faith.

Once again, I got mad.

I immediately started to fast and pray in that hospital. The doctors began to do testing to find out what exactly was going on.

I laid my hands on Maddy's little body and imparted the healing power of God into her.

Every time the doctors ran a test, positive they had found the issue, it would come back negative and they would go back to the drawing board. God was doing what no man could do.

Finally, the doctor came and told us that they had to release Maddy because she was completely fine. They couldn't find anything wrong with her. They couldn't even diagnose her with anything! She was completely healed by the power of God.

She needs no heart specialists to keep and eye on her, she needs no medication to regulate her and she is full of the power of the Holy Spirit!

We left that place rejoicing that God had laid His hand on her body and answered our prayers.

There is nothing like the wonderful power of God! Always remember that God is not just able to bless you, He is also willing to bless you. The Bible says:

> *Now all glory to God, who is able, through his mighty power at work within us, to accomplish infinitely more than we might ask or think.*
>
> *Ephesians 3:20*

I'm encouraging you to start believing for God to accomplish big things in your life. Believe for miracles that are so large that they cannot be ignored.

We have to start asking bigger. Petition Him to do something that will be evident in your life. Something you can use as a testimony of His power.

One of the main reasons people don't receive the power of God in their lives is because they don't ask Him (James 4:2).

A request is a sign of expectation. You don't pull up to a bank drive-through and order a hamburger and fries for the simple reason that you understand the bank doesn't sell fast food.

When you pull through a fast-food drive-through, however, you will place an order because you know what they have available.

Many people don't ask God to perform miracles on their behalf because they don't believe He would do it for them.

Asking Him is a step of faith that says, "Lord I believe that You *can* do it and that You *will* do it."

As His power begins to operate in your everyday life, get ready for an influx of Heaven's joy to follow.

Your days of feeling like you're on the outside looking in are over. You will not have to stand on the fringe while everyone else is rejoicing in their supernatural blessings.

Today is a day to realize that God has prepared wonderful blessings that He will miraculously transfer into your account (1 Corinthians 2:9).

The Apostle Peter said it best when he realized the nature of the God we serve.

> *Then Peter replied, "I see very clearly that God shows no favoritism."*
> **Acts 10:34**

God doesn't pick and choose those to whom He will minister. He searches the earth for faith and when He finds it He rewards it (Hebrews 11:6).

Receive the joy that is embedded in your miracles!

....

"It won't be our resemblance to those who don't have Jesus that will cause them to be changed, but how differ-ent we are."

....

CHAPTER ELEVEN

HIDE THE FIRE EXTINGUISHERS

....

"Therefore God, your God, has anointed you,
pouring out the oil of joy on you more than on anyone else."
—PSALM 45:7

Joy is spiritual. It originates with the Holy Spirit, thus it is spiritually received. Though some of the steps to overwhelming joy that I have written about seem like they are natural, they are spiritual transactions.

When God gives you an instruction and you obey it, you are entering into a spiritual transaction no matter how mundane it may seem. In fact, God can prompt you to do something that doesn't even seem out of the ordinary — and then provide you an extraordinary result.

A perfect example is found in the epilogue of the Gospel of John after Jesus had died and was resurrected.

Peter, who was a fisherman by trade, decided one night to go fishing and six other disciples accompanied him. They got into their boat and began to fish.

The Bible says that they literally fished all night long until the dawn and caught nothing. As they were coming back toward the shore Jesus was standing there, but they didn't recognize Him.

"Fellows, have you caught any fish?" He shouted.

"No," they replied.

"Throw your net on the right side of the boat and you'll get some!" Jesus said. They obeyed and when they did they couldn't haul in the net because there were so many fish in it (John 21:1-6).

Are we to believe that Peter, who was a competent professional fisherman, couldn't find any fish all night because they had been hiding on the right side of his boat?

No.

When Jesus gave them the instruction to throw their net to the other side of the boat He was giving them an opportunity to enter into a spiritual transaction.

There was nothing supernatural about dropping the net into the water. It was their obedience to the Lord's instruction that caused a supernatural result.

It is my belief that those fish were not in the water until Jesus spoke the command and caused them to be created for the disciples to catch.

In the same way, the supernatural result of overwhelming joy in your life can come from simple obedience to the instructions of God's Word.

DIRECT CONNECTION

Since joy is spiritual, it can be spiritually imparted or transferred by the anointing of God. In the same way that healing can be supernaturally released to the sick, joy can be released to those who need it.

The Bible refers to joy as an anointing. Throughout the Word of God oil is used as a symbol of the Holy Spirit or the anointing of God.

In the Old Testament the priests were anointed with oil by Moses as a sign that they were consecrated for the work of the Lord (Exodus 29:7).

In the New Testament we are still instructed to anoint the sick with oil and pray for their healing (James 5:14).

Look what the Psalmist says prophetically of the ministry of Christ:

> *Therefore God, your God, has anointed you, pouring out the oil of joy on you more than on anyone else.*
>
> *Psalm 45:7*

It is so important to understand that joy is received in the presence of God. His anointing will deposit into your spirit what He desires you to have.

I remember the first time that I experienced the wonderful anointing of joy. I was attending Bible school at Rhema Bible Training Center in Tulsa, Oklahoma.

Each February, the school hosted their Winter Bible Seminar.

Brother Kenneth E. Hagin, who was the president of the school and a powerful man of God, ministered each night.

On Tuesday night, as he was trying to preach his message, it seemed as though the Holy Spirit was moving in another direction. We could feel the power of God moving through the auditorium.

Realizing what was happening and yielding to the Holy Spirit, Brother Hagin left the pulpit and walked down onto the main floor. He quoted Psalm 126 and as he did the power of the Holy Spirit began to manifest in the service.

People started laughing and dancing under the anointing of the Spirit of God. As Brother Hagin began to lay hands on different people in the crowd the glory of God shook that service.

Thousands of people were all laughing and rejoicing at the same time. Nothing funny was happening. Nobody prompted us to laugh. We were simply receiving the "oil of joy" that the Bible speaks of in Psalm 45.

The anointing was so strong in the building that even though hands were never laid on me, I fell to the ground under the power of God and began to laugh supernaturally.

I received something from the Lord that night that will never leave me. A supernatural strength that cannot be contained. I became intoxicated with heavenly joy.

SPIRITUAL INTOXICATION

This type of behavior is odd to some people. They don't understand why it's necessary.

There is a very important principle we need to be aware of regarding ourselves. Every human being is a vessel or a container. Whether we realize it or not, we as vessels are designed to be filled with substance.

> *But in a great house there are not only vessels of gold and silver, but also of wood and clay, some for honor and some for dishonor. Therefore if anyone cleanses himself from the latter, he will be a vessel for honor, sanctified and useful for the Master, prepared for every good work.*
>
> *2 Timothy 2:20,21 NKJV*

Have you ever stopped to consider how vast the human spirit is? According to the Gospel of Mark, Jesus confronted a demon-possessed man. When He asked the man's name the demons responded, "My name is Legion, because there are many of us inside this man."

At that time a Roman legion, as the spirit was referring to, consisted of 5,400 soldiers. This man's spirit was vast enough to contain all of those spirits! When Jesus cast them out they filled 2,000 pigs and sent them running off the side of a cliff (Mark 5:1-13).

Everyone will be filled with something, it's up to us to decide what substance that will be. We can either carry the substance of the Holy Spirit or the substances of this natural world.

I find it interesting that when the Holy Spirit was given to the Church on the Day of Pentecost, whatever was happening caused onlookers to assume that the believers were intoxicated! (Acts 2:13).

It was Peter who stood up and said, "These people are not drunk, as some of you are assuming. Nine o'clock in the morning is much too early for that. No, what you see was predicted long ago by the prophet Joel: 'In the last days,' God says, 'I will pour out my Spirit upon all people . . ." (Acts 2:15-17).

These believers had become intoxicated with the power of the Holy Spirit.

When I first began to study the book of Ephesians I came across a passage that confused me until I understood it in the light of Acts chapter 2. The verse says:

> **Don't be drunk with wine, because that will ruin your life. Instead, be filled with the Holy Spirit,**
>
> **Ephesians 5:18**

That seemed like a weird comparison to me. What do these two things have to do with each other? I began to realize that the Apostle Paul was instructing the Church to be intoxicated with the Holy Spirit.

The New Oxford American Dictionary defines intoxicated as: *to cause (someone) to lose control of their faculties or behavior.*[12]

This is a powerful thought because it shows us that being filled with the Spirit allows us to lose control of our natural behaviors and allow ourselves to be controlled by the Holy Spirit of God.

CHOOSE YOUR CHURCH WISELY

Is it possible to be a Christian and not have the joy of the Lord operating in your life? Sure, but why would you want that to be the case?

That is why you must take great care regarding which church you plant yourself in. Not all churches are created equal for the simple reason that not every leader believes the same things about the Bible.

I'm not writing this to attack or promote any specific church, rather, to encourage this generation to place value on the manifestations of the Holy Spirit.

In some churches there is discussion among the leadership about how much of the Holy Spirit to allow in their services as to not frighten visitors and newcomers. They are deciding whether or not they should save those experiences for more intimate settings.

We must understand that the Holy Spirit is not some ethereal cloud or spiritual bird. He is a person and as such He has feelings. He can be grieved (Ephesians 4:30).

Can you imagine if you said to your husband or wife, "Listen, on Sunday morning I'd prefer you don't sit with me in church or even speak to me. I don't want visitors to see that you and I are together. Maybe when we have a smaller gathering where everyone knows each other we can sit together and resume our relationship."

Your spouse would be hurt and you would more than likely have a new permanent sleeping arrangement — the couch.

Remember, true love is never ashamed! The Holy Spirit is our best friend. Without His presence and help we could accomplish nothing. We need Him now more than ever.

If you needed healing because of a terminal disease you wouldn't want to surround yourself with people who continually told you that healing is not for today.

In the same way it is important to join yourself to a body of believers who are not ashamed of the wonderful gifts the Holy Spirit has given to the Church.

> *Always be joyful. Never stop praying. Be*
> *thankful in all circumstances, for this is*
> *God's will for you who belong to Christ*
> *Jesus. Do not stifle the holy spirit.*
> *1 Thessalonians 5:16-19*

Wait a second. I thought that the Holy Spirit can just do whatever He wants to do. No. He needs people to be yielded to His direction and power. We can stifle or quench the Spirit of God by not allowing Him to do what He wants to do.

The Greek word for stifle here is *sbennumi*, meaning *to extinguish*. We must be careful not to extinguish the fire of the Holy Spirit or become embarrassed of His presence in our lives.

The purpose of the Holy Spirit is to draw men and women to Jesus and build the Church. The Early Church described in the book of Acts, which was filled with the manifestations and miracles of the Holy Spirit, never had an issue with church growth. Thousands were added to the Church daily!

Position yourself in a place where the joy of the Holy Spirit can operate in your life. Religion kills, whereas relationship with the Spirit of God brings life and strength! (2 Corinthians 3:6).

This is a generation that will not be changed by the impotent forms and customs of nominal church, but by the visible power of God that can rearrange every broken situation in their lives.

It's time to hide the fire extinguishers and allow the Holy Spirit to move the way He wants to. It won't be our resemblance to those who don't have Jesus that will cause them to be changed, but how different we are.

The Holy Spirit is releasing strength and power to His people. Let us be the generation that embraces it.

PART 3

THE BENEFITS PACKAGE

When you're living in overwhelming joy it opens the door to a whole new realm of supernatural possibilities.

....

"God's instructions for our personal lives are the keys that unlock His provision and divine help."

....

CHAPTER TWELVE
CAN YOU HEAR ME NOW?

"With joy you will draw water from the
wells of salvation."
—ISAIAH 12:3

Now that you're walking in the power of overwhelming joy, get ready to reap the rewards. There are wonderful benefits attached to living as God designed you to live.

One of the things that becomes readily evident is that it's much easier to hear the voice of God when your soul is not weighted down with depression and anxiety.

When you're battling through a crisis it's extremely hard to focus on anything else than what you are dealing with. Although our walk of faith encourages us to push past our natural emotions to receive what God has prepared for us spiritually, it becomes a simple task when you are full of Heaven's happiness.

You may remember a series of television commercials launched by Verizon Wireless touting the power and coverage of their cellular network. In the ads, actor Paul Marcarelli would walk onto different sets in his staple Verizon maintenance coat holding a cell phone to his ear and asking the question, "Can you hear me now?"

When you receive freedom from the weight of the natural world, it's as though God is asking you the same question.

Can you hear Me now?

I'm sure you've been places where you've had to move around to locate a stronger cellular signal. You've stood by a window or a door. Maybe you've had to go outside to make the call.

The wonderful joy of the Holy Spirit positions you to have a clear connection with the voice of God. The Bible says:

> **With joy you will draw water from the wells of salvation.**
> **Isaiah 12:3 NKJV**

Your salvation contains many wells that are filled with the resources of God. The wells contain health, strength, wisdom, blessing and peace, just to name a few. One of the most important resources found in the wells of salvation are your personal instructions from God.

God has a wonderful plan and dynamic purpose for

every believer. If you never discover God's will for your life, your journey to Heaven will prove a frustrating one.

God's instructions for our personal lives are the keys that unlock His provision and divine help.

In the Gospels, Jesus attached purpose to His disciples by giving them instructions and a mission. After they returned from accomplishing their purpose, Jesus asked them if they ever found themselves in lack, to which they replied, "no" (Luke 22:35).

Your instructions and purpose are available—inside the wells of your salvation. Notice that they cannot be extracted in the absence of joy.

Joy is the bucket that draws out the contents of your wells. Even if you had a multimillion dollar home filled with the best food available, you could starve if you didn't have the key to get inside.

Every believer has been afforded the blessings of God, but we can only receive them by the means that God has provided.

PROPHETIC PITY PARTY

Elijah was one of the most famous prophets in the entire Bible. He stood on top of Mount Carmel and had a showdown with the prophets of Baal.

He called fire down from Heaven and it proved that our God is the only true God.

This is the same man that could slap a body of water with his coat and the water would part so he could walk across on dry ground.

When it was time for him to leave the earth, God sent a special chariot of fire to come and pick him up and take him into Heaven. He was one of the only two men in the Old Testament who didn't have to die to get to Heaven. (The other was Enoch.)

So we're not talking about some little novice who didn't know what he was doing. This was a pro. Elijah was one of God's main men on the earth.

However, even Elijah had to gain victory over depression and anxiety before God could continue using him.

After Elijah finished calling fire down from Heaven and slaughtering all of the false prophets of Baal, the king and his wife, Jezebel, vowed to kill him.

He was afraid and fled to a town called Beersheba. From there he escaped into the wilderness until he finally collapsed under a juniper tree exhausted, afraid, and depressed.

"I have had enough, Lord," he said. "Take my life, for I am no better than my ancestors who have already died." Then he laid down and slept under the juniper tree.

God's man of faith and power was so distraught by what was going on, and had fallen so deeply into depression, that he was ready to die.

God wasn't finished using Elijah, but He couldn't use him in that state. Before God could continue to allow Elijah's destiny to unfold, He had to encourage him.

The encouragement of God will always invigorate your purpose.

God sent an angel to wake him up, feed him, and give him supernatural strength for his journey. Next, God showed His power to Elijah again just to remind him what He could do. Finally, God encouraged Elijah when he felt isolated. Elijah thought he was the only one left serving God, but God revealed that there were thousands of people remaining who refused to bow their knees to any other gods.

As soon as Elijah received supernatural encouragement and was delivered from his depression, God began giving him fresh instructions and renewed purpose (1 Kings 19:1-18).

Joy is such a dynamic force that it propels you into the spiritual current of Heaven's agenda.

If the devil can't kill you, his next best option is to keep you stranded in a place where you cannot produce fruit for the kingdom of God.

He wants you stuck, unable to accomplish your purpose. Joy is the wonderful remedy of the Holy Spirit.

GLASS HALF FULL . . . OF MANURE

While I'm not talking merely about optimism or a positive attitude, when you're walking in the overwhelming joy of the Spirit, these things will follow.

I once heard a parable regarding this principle. A few years ago a major research project was commissioned by a world-renowned university. The purpose of the study was to objectively develop operational definitions for pessimists and optimists for use in textbooks, academic papers, and classroom learning.

The scientists, behaviorists, and psychologists involved scoured the globe searching for the most pessimistic and optimistic people they could find. Their key objective was to bring test subjects back to the lab for further study. After a year of looking, the team finally narrowed their search down to two eight-year-old boys.

Back at the lab, two observation rooms were readied. The first room was filled with every kind of toy imaginable. There were so many toys that it seemed to the researchers that an entire toy store had been emptied for the sake of the study. The second room was filled wall-to-wall with horse manure. The boys were to each be placed in a room and their behaviors would be observed from behind one-way mirrors.

The first little boy stood skeptically in the doorway of the room full of toys, not sure if he should enter. But with a little prodding from one of the researchers who said, "Go on in, they are all yours," he finally walked over to the first toy. What happened next shocked and stunned the researchers. Instead of playing gleefully the little boy systematically opened every single package in the room and rejected each of the toys in turn. The researchers heard him whining: "These aren't like my toys at home. These toys will never work. Where are the video games? Its hot in here. I don't have any friends to play with."

The complaining went on and on until soon, exhausted from his own negativity, he sat down in the middle of the room and with a big pout on his face he angrily shouted, "I'm bored and I want to go home."

The researchers had been so mesmerized by this display of pessimism and negativity that they had almost forgotten about the second little boy who had been placed in the room full of manure.

They quickly shifted their attention to the second room. Peering through the observation window, they were astonished. They had expected to see the little boy sitting on the pile, sad and crying. Instead, he was standing on top of the pile wildly shoveling horse manure. To the amazement of the entire research team, he was animated, excited, alive, and happy. He kept digging and digging and shouting with glee. He was covered with manure from head to toe and he was ecstatic. The researchers looked at one another in awe — the child seemed delirious.

Cautiously, one of the scientists opened the door to the room and tried to get the boy's attention. However, he was so focused on digging that it took a few minutes to do so.

Finally, the boy stopped what he was doing, turned around, and faced the scientist. Looking with amazement at the manure covered child the researcher asked, "Son, what in the world are you doing?"

A huge grin crossed the boy's face and with the same enthusiasm he had given to digging he replied, "Sir, with all this manure I just know there is pony in here somewhere and I'm going to find him!" With that he turned around and resumed digging.

Joy allows you to attack any situation with a supernatural energy that cannot be explained by human intellect. It sets you apart from the crowd. It causes you to produce at a higher level because of the supernatural strength that accompanies it.

This is a spiritual principle that is now being understood by the scientific community. Your ability to focus and retain knowledge is greatly hindered by depression and anxiety. In fact, Dr. Charles Raison, an associate professor of psychiatry and behavioral sciences at Emory University wrote:

"Problems with focusing and remembering are classic depressive symptoms . . . anything that makes your depression go away will fix your cognitive difficulties precisely because they are part of the depression."[13]

THE MYTH OF ACCOMPLISHMENT-BASED JOY

Joy allows you to supernaturally focus on what God has called you to do and accomplish your purpose with accuracy. For too long, we've been taught that when we succeed, our accomplishment will bring the joy we want.

The problem with this train of thought is it would have you believe that you can't access joy until you've reached the end of accomplishment.

If this were true, you wouldn't be empowered to accomplish your purpose until your purpose was already accomplished.

That makes no sense.

Joy is not waiting for you at the end of the tunnel of success. Rather, it is the necessary fuel that carries you to your expected end. King David understood this perfectly and wrote in a Psalm to the Lord:

> *Restore to me the joy of your salvation,*
> *and make me willing to obey you. Then*
> *I will teach your ways to the rebels, and*
> *they will return to you.*
>
> *Psalm 51:12,13*

Notice that the joy of his salvation wasn't coming after he accomplished his work for the Lord. He knew that the joy of his salvation would first be restored empowering him to pursue his purpose for God.

IT'S YOUR RESPONSIBILITY TO CARRY BLESSINGS. IT'S GOD'S RESPONSIBILITY TO CARRY BURDENS.

His prayer points out that joy would enable him to hear the commands of God and then obey them.

Make up your mind right now that you will no longer be bogged down by the weight of your enemy. You will receive the mighty joy of the Holy Spirit and hear the voice of God as He speaks directly to you.

From this moment forward you will draw fresh water from the wells of salvation every single day.

You should expect to see God expedite His plan for your life as your worries begin to vanish. You were not built to shoulder your own burdens. As a believer, you are mandated to function as a conveyor belt. As soon as the cares of this world are laid on your shoulders, immediately transfer them onto God.

It's your responsibility to carry blessings. It's God's responsibility to carry burdens (1 Peter 5:7).

This is the avenue that leads to feather-light living for the Lord.

"The devil can't stop God from giving you a divine purpose, so his plan is to rob you of strength so you can't fulfill it."

CHAPTER THIRTEEN

HEAVEN'S RED BULL

"Don't be dejected and sad, for
the joy of the Lord is your strength!"
—NEHEMIAH 8:10

Every believer that ever lived has been given a divine purpose by God. We are each called to accomplish something different for the kingdom of Heaven and there is no such thing as a member of the body of Christ who is useless.

Think for a moment about what God has called you to do. Consider the dreams He has placed in your heart. It takes strength and faith to accomplish your purpose on the earth.

This is important to remember when the enemy makes an attempt to rob you of joy. The devil doesn't mind if you laugh once in awhile as long as overflowing joy isn't a part of your lifestyle. (Proverbs 14:13)

The primary reason that the enemy attacks your joy

is so that he can rob you of strength. He knows that he cannot stop God from giving you a purpose and a destiny, so his plan is simply to steal your strength so that you don't fulfill your divine calling.

The joy of the Lord is like a supernatural energy drink. It empowers you to run your race with momentum! It allows you to operate with God's own strength. Look what the Word of God says:

> *. . . Don't be dejected and sad, for the joy of the Lord is your strength!*
> *Nehemiah 8:10*

I find it interesting that the Hebrew word for strength here means a *"fortress of defense."* God uses the peace and joy of His Holy Spirit to defend your mind and body from the natural effects of this world.

> *. . . His peace will guard your hearts and minds as you live in Christ Jesus.*
> *Philippians 4:7*

HEAVEN'S HEALTH CARE PLAN

According to the Anxiety and Depression Association of America:

- Anxiety disorders are the most common mental illness in America affecting 18% of the population.
- People with an anxiety disorder are three to five times more likely to go to the doctor and six times more likely to be hospitalized for psychiatric disorders than those who do not suffer from anxiety disorders.
- More than 1 in 10 Americans take antidepressants, the primary type of medication used by people ages 18-44.[14]

It is clear than the devil is using depression and anxiety to destroy the minds and bodies of people around the world. The book of Proverbs shows us the stark contrast between these two ways of living.

> *A cheerful heart is good medicine, but a broken spirit saps a person's strength.*
> *Proverbs 17:22*

The King James Version of this verse says that *"a broken spirit dries the bones."* Depression and anxiety are demonic attacks against the people of God! Depression is never something that any believer should be satisfied to live with. We should treat it not as a normal effect of life, but as an enemy of our destiny.

How do we combat the heaviness that the devil attempts to use against us? It is only by walking in the joy of the Holy Spirit that we can live an overcoming life. Joy is one of Heaven's prescribed medications. It is impossible to be an effective, productive member of the kingdom without it's operation in your life.

Dr. Paul E. McGhee, a pioneer in humor research who published over 50 scientific articles and 13 books on humor wrote, "Your sense of humor is one of the most powerful tools you have to make certain that your daily mood and emotional state support good health."[15]

Science is finally catching up with the truth of God's Word. A merry heart does good like a medicine! God wants you to have the strength to carry out your purpose efficiently and with power.

THE HEALING MINISTRY OF THE THREE STOOGES

In the early 1990s a minister who is a friend of our family called my father. He had been pastoring a church, and the enemy was attacking his mind and his family using the pressures of ministry along with unloving people who were continually criticizing him.

He seemed on the verge of a breakdown when he

called my father for advice and help. My father encouraged him to come down to our home and stay with us for a week to rest and be refreshed.

When he arrived my father had a plan. Every night after dinner we would go into the living room and my dad would put on The Three Stooges, Abbott and Costello and other comedies. That pastor sat in the recliner and just laughed and laughed the entire week.

That doesn't sound very spiritual, I can hear some of you thinking. It wasn't. It was Moe poking Curly in the eye and hitting Larry in the head with a cast iron skillet, but the key was the transformation of a broken spirit into a merry heart.

He left our house the next week with a freedom in his spirit that was not previously there. Breakthrough had come to him through the power of joy. Today, over twenty years later, that man is still preaching the gospel, his ministry is expanding and he is doing better than he has ever done! Joy gives you supernatural momentum to accomplish your purpose.

Too often people spend all of their time focusing on the negative things that the devil is trying to do in their lives rather than enjoying life and laughing even in the face of adversity.

How could we ever laugh in a time of trouble? We have to realize that it's not our job to take care of ourselves. It is God's job to take care of us! The Apostle Peter said it perfectly. Let's look at it in the Amplified Bible.

> *Casting the whole of your care [all your anxieties, all your worries, all your concerns, once and for all] on Him, for He cares for you affectionately and cares about you watchfully.*
>
> *1 Peter 5:7 AMP*

Your Heavenly Father is constantly watching out for you and making sure that He is taking care of you. Some people give some of their concerns to God and keep some for themselves. However, this verse makes it clear than not one of your issues truly belongs to you.

GOD'S DIVINE CARRIER

In 2010, my wife Carolyn and I had our first daughter, Madelyn. We got a baby carrier and brought it to the hospital with us. The day they allowed us to take her home from the hospital a massive snow storm hit Virginia Beach and we had ten inches of snow on the ground.

We wrapped her up tight and strapped her into her

carrier and began driving home. I was so nervous to drive with a baby in the car I probably drove 12 mph the entire way home. Madelyn just slept in the carrier.

For the next several weeks, when she would wake up in her crib in the morning she would just lie there until we came to get her out. I would get her dressed and put her in the carrier and we'd go wherever we needed to go and she looked like she didn't have a care in the world.

When it was time to eat, we would just put her into her high chair and feed her. I started noticing a pattern. I never walked into her room and found her in the crib worrying about how our family was going to get the money to buy her baby clothes. I never found her depressed about gas prices or the rising cost of groceries.

As a baby, Madelyn's understanding was, *If my dad is there then my food will be there. If my dad is there then my clothes will be there. If my dad is there then he will put me into the carrier and take me where I need to go.*

When I realized that I gained full understanding of what this verse meant. I heard the Lord say, "I want my people to stop worrying about how they will make things come together in their lives and just get into my divine carrier and let me take them where I want them to go!"

When we allow God to carry us into our purpose we gain access to His momentum. He supernaturally carries us to the destination He planned. The best part is that when we arrive our energy isn't depleted from the journey!

It can be frustrating to work at something that is not your specific assignment and never see the promotion of Heaven on your life. That's why the Bible says:

> **Unless the Lord builds a house, the work of the builders is wasted. Unless the Lord protects a city, guarding it with sentries will do no good.**
> **Psalm 127:1**

It's impossible to attain overwhelming joy when you are not accomplishing your God-given purpose. That is why the story of Nehemiah is so relevant as we discuss the connection between your joy and your purpose. Nehemiah relates his story to us this way:

> Early the following spring, in the month of Nisan, during the twentieth year of King Artaxerxes' reign, I was serving the king his wine. I had never before appeared sad in his presence. So the king asked me, 'Why are you looking so sad? You don't look sick to me. You must be deeply troubled.'

Then I was terrified, but I replied, 'Long live the king! How can I not be sad? For the city where my ancestors are buried is in ruins, and the gates have been destroyed by fire.'

The king asked, 'Well, how can I help you?'

With a prayer to the God of heaven, I replied, 'If it please the king, and if you are pleased with me, your servant, send me to Judah to rebuild the city where my ancestors are buried.' (Nehemiah 2:1-5)

This is the same guy who later encouraged the people of Judah not to be dejected and sad because the joy of the Lord was their strength. What was the determining factor that transformed him from a sad servant standing in front of his king to an effective leader encouraging others to have supernatural joy? It was the fact that he began accomplishing his purpose on the earth.

Nehemiah's destiny was not to stand and pour the king's wine. His destiny was to rebuild the walls of Judah for the Lord. It weighed heavily upon his heart and restricted his joy until he began to do what he was called to do.

When we produce fruit for God's kingdom it allows

us to access the free-flowing joy of Heaven.

I MIGHT BE DUMB . . . BUT I'M NOT STUPID

It is vital we understand that issues like depression, anxiety and fear are not natural; rather, they are supernatural problems that should be supernaturally addressed. That is why Paul said:

> *For we are not fighting against flesh-and-blood enemies, but against evil rulers and authorities of the unseen world, against mighty powers in this dark world, and against evil spirits in the heavenly places.*
>
> *Ephesians 6:12*

As long as we believe that these issues are just normal struggles of life that everyone just has to deal with in their own way, we will miss the opportunity to live on a higher plane where victory is commonplace.

We have to recognize these evil weapons of the devil for what they are. When we become complacent with aspects of our lives not instituted by God, we will not attempt change. This is the reason that many people won't alter their unhealthy eating habits until they have caused sickness and disease and a doctor insists upon change.

Don't wait until your purpose has been thwarted and you've run out of steam before you combat these attacks of the enemy in your life!

I've heard people dismiss these things as being hormonal or the result of a diagnosed condition that they just cannot control.

There is no natural condition that is not alterable by supernatural forces!

It is time that we as God's people realize what the enemy is attempting to do so that we can stand in our authority as Paul encouraged the Corinthian hurch:

> *so that no advantage would be taken of us by Satan, for we are not ignorant of his schemes.*
> ### 2 Corinthians 2:11 NASB

Truth is flooding your life and your days of tears and weakness have come to an end. Welcome to your personal victory — Heaven on earth.

....

"Joy is a fuel that propels you, peace allows you to hear the directions to your destination."

....

CHAPTER FOURTEEN
SILENCE THE RABBLE

*"Then you will experience God's peace, which exceeds
anything we can understand. His peace will guard
your hearts and minds as you live in Christ Jesus."*
—PHILIPPIANS 4:7

When I was a youth pastor our youth group would play
a game. I would pick a guy and a girl from the audience
to stand up and we would blindfold them.

We would place a prize in the back of the room that
they had to find without being able to see. So how would
they get there? When the game began the other guys
and girls in the youth group would shout out directions
to the blindfolded students . . . all at the same time.

It was pandemonium.

It's hard to get your directions when everyone is
shouting at you all at once. To make it more confusing,
the guys would give wrong directions to the girl who
was blindfolded and vice versa. They wanted their team
to win the prize.

Imagine being the student who was blindfolded. You've been spun around until you're dizzy and disoriented, and you hear tons of people shouting at you about what you should do next and you can't quite figure out which voice to listen to.

It's extremely difficult. Many times we would laugh as people bumped into walls and chairs trying to reach the prize.

It's not like they were in an obstacle course. It was our normal youth room that they had seen hundreds of times. They just couldn't navigate through the confusion.

IT TAKES THE PEACE OF GOD TO BE PROPERLY LED INTO THE WONDERFUL DESTINY THAT GOD HAS FOR YOU.

The same is true in our own lives. Unless God opens our eyes to see the invisible, we can't look into the supernatural realm. We've got to be led to our next appointment by the Holy Spirit.

Without the peace of God, your mind is filled with thousands of thoughts and voices shouting at you trying to bring confusion and cause you to miss out on what God has planned for your life.

It takes the peace of God to be properly led into the wonderful destiny that God has for you.

Joy and peace go hand-in-hand. In fact, to have the peace of God ruling your life, you must also have the joy of the Holy Spirit.

They have two different applications. Joy is a fuel that propels you, while peace allows you to hear the directions to your destination. The Bible says:

> *"For you will go out with joy And be led forth with peace;*
>
> ### Isaiah 55:12 NASB

Imagine how easy that game would have been if I refused to allow any other students to make any noise and I gave specific directions that led directly to the prize. There would be no point in playing the game because the challenge would be removed.

In the same way, when joy and peace silence the rabble, the challenge of following the voice of God becomes easy.

David made it clear in Psalm 23 that God leads us beside still waters. Still waters are representative of peace. God isn't just randomly leading us, He leads us to peace and not into anxiety or panic.

I imagine some of you are thinking, *What about the battles we face in life?* It's true that we are called to fight the good fight of faith and lay hold on eternal life (1 Timothy 6:12). However, just because you're engaged in a fight doesn't mean that you have a reason to lose your peace.

On the contrary, the moments when your faith is put to the test are the perfect times to operate in absolute peace. Once again, that is the true essence of faith.

ELISHA AND THE FIERY HORSE BRIGADE

There was a war raging between Israel and Aram. The king of Aram called his counselors and generals into his chamber to plan their attacks.

Their tacticians began to devise battle plans to assault the nation of Israel and their troops. Every time they would solidify their plans, however, God would reveal them to the prophet Elisha.

Elisha would then warn the regions of Israel that were about to be attacked and the attack would fail.

The king of Aram was furious. He was positive that there was a traitor among his inner circle of advisors. Finally, he called them all together and demanded to know who was betraying him.

"It's not us, lord king," one of the officers replied. "Elisha, the prophet in Israel, tells the king of Israel even the words you speak in the privacy of your own bedroom!"

"Go and find out where he is," the king commanded, "So I can send troops to seize him."

The report came back with information on the exact location of Elisha. The king sent a great army with many chariots and horses to surround the city where Elisha was staying.

When Elisha's servant woke up early the next morning and went outside, there were troops, horses and chariots everywhere.

"Oh, sir, what will we do now?" The young man cried to Elisha.

"Don't be afraid!" Elisha told him. "For there are more on our side than on theirs!"

Then Elisha prayed, "Oh Lord, open his eyes and let him see!" The Lord opened the young man's eyes, and when he looked up, he saw that the hillside around Elisha was filled with horses and chariots of fire.

They went on to easily subdue their enemies that day because the Lord fought for them (2 Kings 6:8-16).

I find it interesting that Elisha knew what was happening that day and showed no signs of nervousness or panic. It was his servant who had the spiritual blindfold on.

No doubt hundreds of fearful thoughts ran through the servant's mind that morning when he caught sight of the enemy's army surrounding the city.

I'm sure he was tempted to pack his bags and run for his life while the prophet was still sleeping.

It was the prayer that Elisha prayed that allowed the servant to lose his anxiety and step into supernatural peace that morning.

There is an abundance of joy knowing that you're not alone, but God is fighting for you.

KEEP CALM AND CARRY ON

Nowadays, we see the "Keep Calm and Carry On" slogan modified and slapped on any product hoping to be sold. Sometimes it's used as a funny catchphrase on t-shirts, most unfortunately: "Keep Calm and Eat Chocolate" or "Keep Calm and Avoid Zombies."

However, "Keep Calm and Carry On" was a slogan on a motivational poster produced by the British government in 1939 in preparation for the Second World War. The poster was intended to raise the morale of the British public.

It was produced as part of a series of three "Home Publicity" posters. (The others read "Your Courage, Your Cheerfulness, Your Resolution Will Bring Us Victory" and "Freedom Is In Peril. Defend It With All Your Might.")

Each poster showed the slogan under a representation of a "Tudor Crown" which was a symbol of the state. They were intended to be distributed in order to strengthen morale in the event of a wartime disaster. It was widely expected that within hours of an outbreak of war, major cities would suffer mass bombings using high explosives and poison gas.

In a time of extreme danger and uncertainty, the British were encouraged to have peace. I don't know if that is possible to the natural mind, but the Word of God encourages us to do the very same thing with spiritual help:

> *And the peace of God, which surpasses all understanding, will guard your hearts and minds through Christ Jesus.*
> *Philippians 4:7 NKJV*

The peace of God surpasses all human understanding because it is activated in times when you shouldn't have any peace.

It may look like you are surrounded by enemies on every side and the forces of darkness have gathered against you. There is no logical reason to have peace in that situation, but the promises of God are impenetrable by your enemy. This is one of the most powerfully worded promises in God's Word:

> *Do not be afraid of the terrors of the night*

> *. . . Do not dread the disease that stalks in darkness . . . Though a thousand fall at your side, though ten thousand are dying around you, these evils will not touch you.*
>
> *Psalm 91:5-7*

So take your spiritual blindfold off. The joy of the Lord has afforded you supernatural peace. The thoughts and voices that plagued you in the past must now stay silent. Joy is propelling you into your wonderful destiny and peace is directing you to the prize.

The days of you floundering from one temporary remedy to another are over.

THE LONELINESS TRAP

One of the schemes of the devil is to isolate you and make you feel like you're alone. Loneliness is a condition that can cause anxiety and panic robbing you of peace.

The danger of trying to solve loneliness on your own is the trap that Satan wants you to fall into. Logically, people feel like they need more interaction so they attempt to use events, gatherings, and time with their friends as a substitute for what they really need—the presence of the Holy Spirit.

Loneliness is a plot of the devil to constantly surround you with distractions that keep you from fellowship with God. Once again, we must understand that fullness of joy can only be found in the presence of God (Psalm 16:11).

Jesus, the epitome of a man filled with peace, gives us a visual demonstration of how he unlocked the peace of Heaven in His own life — He often got away by Himself to pray (Luke 5:16). In fact, sometimes Jesus would spend many hours alone seeking the face of God because He understood that He could only give to others what He had already received from His Father in prayer.

Our generation has plenty of meaningless distractions immediately available to us. We don't need more social stimulation; we need to access our supernatural connection to the voice of our Heavenly Father.

Set aside time in your schedule to be alone in the presence of God and receive fresh updates from Heaven. Therein lies your peace and strength.

The peace and rest you need cannot come from natural sources. There is a peace that is set aside for you by God. The Psalmist said it best:

God gives rest to His loved ones.

Psalm 127:2

....

"Submerge yourself in the Word and anxiety, worry, and depression are washed away by the forceful current of Living Water."

....

STOP READING. START EATING.

···

"Your words were found, and I ate them,
And Your word was to me the joy and rejoicing of my heart;"
—JEREMIAH 15:16

Fall had come to Tulsa, Oklahoma, and with it a new influx of students coming to college. I was one of those students.

I moved to Tulsa at the age of eighteen from a small town in West Virginia that was over a thousand miles away. After settling in to the apartment that I rented to live in, God supernaturally provided a job for me.

Over the first few months of the school year I realized that my schedule was more intense than I thought it would be.

I worked the third shift from 11:00 P.M. until 8:00 A.M. When I was finished I would drive straight to school and attend classes from 8:30 A.M. until 12:00 P.M.

After classes finished I volunteered my time in the

Prayer and Healing School. These services, in which I played the organ and sang with the worship team, were held from 1:00 until about 3:00 each afternoon.

When I was finished with those services I would return home and complete my homework, eat and do anything that needed to be done before going to bed around 5:00 and waking up at 10:00 to start all over again.

Averaging five hours of sleep a night along with my heavy schedule began to wear me out. There was nothing I could eliminate. I was there to attend school, God had spoken to me to assist in the Prayer and Healing School, and I had to work a job.

The Bible says If you don't work, you don't eat (2 Thessalonians 3:10), and anyone who knows me understands how much I like to eat—so there was no way I was going to quit my job.

One afternoon, I was sitting in a class being taught by Kenneth E. Hagin, the president and founder of the school I was attending. I found myself dozing off in class. I shook myself awake and became a bit irritated.

I thought, *Lord, I didn't come all the way down here to work a job or play the organ. I came to receive an impartation from this man and his ministry. So You're going to have to do something to help me out and give me strength.*

I didn't have to wait on God to give me a supernatural answer. In fact, all He did was speak a scripture reference to my spirit. I heard, "Romans 8:11." I didn't even have to turn there. I knew the scripture by heart:

> *The Spirit of God, who raised Jesus from the dead, lives in you. And just as God raised Christ Jesus from the dead, he will give life to your mortal bodies by this same Spirit living within you.*
>
> *Romans 8:11*

The phrase "give life to" in this verse comes from the Greek word *zoopoieo* which literally translated means "to invigorate by spiritual power."

When I received this word from the Holy Spirit, I didn't read the scripture . . . I ate it.

I didn't literally rip the page out of my Bible, chew it up and swallow it. I'm not insane. What I mean is that my spirit man ingested it.

It is possible to read the Bible or hear it preached and not ingest it into your being. That is why although Doubting Thomas traveled with Jesus, listened to Him preach daily and saw Him perform miracles, his faith wasn't built like some of the other disciples. This is why we don't know him as "Believing Thomas."

That word from God became like supernatural nutrition to my physical body. That is one of the attributes of

God's Word. It brings health and strength to you physically (Proverbs 4:20-22).

I began to confess it and thank God that He was supernaturally invigorating my body. From that day forward a supernatural strength and energy came on me. I didn't change my sleeping habits, take vitamins, drink Red Bull or any other supplement.

The Word, when ingested, produced heavenly strength by itself. The Old Testament prophet Jeremiah understood this and said:

> *Your words were found, AND I ATE*
> *THEM, And Your word was to me the joy*
> *and rejoicing of my heart;*
> *Jeremiah 15:16 NKJV*

Only the Word that you receive by faith and ingest in your spirit can be transformed into supernatural joy that fuels your Christian life.

YOUR PERSONAL TREASURE CHEST

The Word of God is a literal cache of overwhelming joy. Jeremiah said that God's word became the joy and rejoicing of his heart.

God's Word deposits into your spirit what nothing

else in the world can. It is an invaluable resource.

It's important to understand that God's Word is not the only source of joy. Although it adds joy to your life, God's Word also requires joy to receive.

In the parable of the sower found in Matthew 13, we see that the seed of God's Word fell on four different types of ground. I only want to draw your attention to one of them.

Thorny ground.

The Bible says when God's Word fell on that type of ground the thorns choked it out and it died. Later, when Jesus was explaining the story, He showed them that the thorns represent the worries and anxieties of life (Matthew 13:22).

The access points I have given you in this book will destroy the depression and anxiety that the enemy has used to destroy you, but then ingesting the Word of God will cause you to continue in that overwhelming joy. The Psalmist said:

> *I rejoice at Your word As one who finds*
> *great treasure.*
>> ***Psalm 119:162 NKJV***

Every time you uncover something new in the Word of God you are qualified to live in a new level of manifestation.

That treasure you uncover is a key that gives you access to new areas of God's kingdom.

DAILY REFRESHING

I remember when my father installed a pool at our house in West Virginia. I didn't swim very often for two reasons. First, I don't care for swimming that much and secondly, because we usually had chilly nights even during the summer, so the water was always freezing.

My use of the pool would come after I would spend the majority of my day playing basketball in the summer heat until I couldn't take it anymore. Then I would jog home and without even changing into a bathing suit, (or out of my basketball shoes) I would run and jump into the pool.

No matter how hot, sweaty and tired I was, in seconds I felt completely refreshed. Submerging myself in the cold water brought instant change.

In the same way, the Apostle Paul tells us that the Word of God is the water that washes over us bringing refreshing and cleansing us (Ephesians 5:26).

As you submerge yourself in the Scripture, all anxiety, worry, depression and confusion are washed away by the forceful current of Living Water.

When we refuse to ingest the mighty Word of God, we deprive our spirits of proper nutrition.

F.F. Bosworth was an American evangelist who ministered during the early twentieth century. He focused on faith and healing and he saw God **MOST CHRISTIANS FEED THEIR BODIES THREE HOT MEALS A DAY AND ONE COLD SNACK A WEEK AND WONDER WHY THEY'RE SO WEAK IN FAITH.** perform many miracles during his ministry.

He was best known for his famous book, *Christ the Healer*, which has over 500,000 copies in print.

In that book he commented on the state of a malnourished spirit when he wrote, "Most Christians feed their bodies three hot meals a day and one cold snack a week and wonder why they're so weak in faith."[16]

That's why when we begin to realize how wonderful and revitalizing the Word of God is, we develop a hunger for it.

It no longer feels like a list of to-dos, but a menu of benefits that has been custom-made for you. That's how I believe the Psalmist felt when he described receiving the Word:

> *How sweet your words taste to me; they are sweeter than honey.*
>
> *Psalm 119:103*

Why did he say that God's Word was so sweet? Because he goes on to explain that they give understanding and guide through all points of life. They were a literal light to his pathway.

The Bible is a book of supernatural solutions. What makes the Scripture sweet is the divine help behind each promise.

The Bible declares regarding God's Word:

> *It is the same with my word. I send it out, and it always produces fruit. It will accomplish all I want it to, and it will prosper everywhere I send it.*
>
> *Isaiah 55:11*

There is nothing in your life that God's Word cannot accomplish. Don't just read it. Don't just hear it. Devour it. Ingest it. Let it bring overwhelming joy to your life.

REPEAT.

I want you to focus on the repeat part of this book's title. Joy is an ever-flowing spiritual fruit. Just like the rest of the fruit of the Spirit, your joy will come under constant attack from the natural order of this world.

It's not enough to just praise God one time or hear

and obey one instruction from the Lord. You can't give once and expect to see the return for the rest of your life.

Dedication to these principles will bring a constant flow of overwhelming joy each and every day. That's why Paul encouraged the Church in Galatia:

> *And let us not grow weary while doing good, for in due season we shall reap if we do not lose heart.*
>
> *Galatians 6:9 NKJV*

I pray that this book has opened your eyes to the fact that your purpose is directly connected to your joy. Joy is not an accident, nor does it have to be temporary.

From this day forward I pray that you will walk forcefully into the greatest days of production for God's kingdom that you've ever known. May your joy fuel your momentum into exceeding greatness.

You've been positioned at the action point of promotion. You're standing today on the riverbank of overwhelming joy. Don't dip your toe in to feel the water.

Jump.

ACKNOWLEDGMENTS

The work of the Holy Spirit is such an amazing thing. His ability to lead and guide never ceases to amaze me. I'm forever thankful for the mighty Baptism of the Holy Spirit that allows me to be led by the voice of God.

Thank you to all of my friends and family who offered support, encouragement, and assistance with this book. I'm especially appreciative of:

Carolyn. My wonderful wife who is always encouraging me to do what I'm called to do with excellence. You are an amazing example of joy and love and I'm blessed to have you.

Madelyn and Brooklyn. My sweet girls whom I love so much. Supernatural joy is already evident in your lives. God's best is yours.

Dad and Mom. The greatest examples of the power of kingdom dedication I know. I love you.

A.E. and Carlene Shuttlesworth. You both created a family legacy of Holy Spirit power. Your prayers and dedication have produced generational fruit.

Tim, Tiff and Terry Shuttlesworth. My uncles who have all poured into my life in countless ways.

Jonathan Shuttlesworth. You were zero help, but you paid for a spot in this section. www.revivaltoday.cc (Promoted)

Stephanie Iaquinto. Your keen eye, vast knowledge and wonderful style suggestions transformed this into a readable manuscript. You wield a red pen as though it were a light saber.

Ramen Noodles. Your sodium-filled goodness fueled many late-night writing sessions.

Those things you stick into the ends of corn on the cob. Thank you for allowing me to eat this summer treat without getting my hands covered in greasy, melted butter.

The homeless guy who stole my iPod. I don't know if you'll get a chance to read this, but I forgive you. But seriously, if I see you snooping around my house again I'll shave your beard with a butter knife.

Hot Topic stores. As a hotbed of depression, anxiety and teen angst, you always give me a starting point to bring deliverance to the captives.

Blockbuster Video. Thank you for closing down before I had to pay back the $7,324 that I owed in late fees. (Every time I rented a movie I expected S.W.A.T. teams to swing in through the windows.)

S.W.A.T. Teams. For not swinging in through Blockbuster's windows.

ENDNOTES

....

1. Compton, Wilson M., M.D., M.P.E., Kevin P. Conway, Ph.D., Frederick S. Stinson, Ph.D., and Bridget F. Grant, Ph.D. "Changes in the Prevalence of Major Depression and Comorbid Substance Use Disorders in the United States Between 1991-1992 and 2001-2002." *The American Journal of Psychiatry* 163.12 (2006): n. pag. Web.
2. Keller, W. Phillip. *A Shepherd Looks at Psalm 23*. Grand Rapids: Zondervan Pub. House, 1970. Print.
3. McManus, Paul. " Prayer Statistics." Prayer Stats. N.p., n.d. Web. 09 May 2014. <http://www.the7greatprayers.com/prayerstats.aspx>.
4. "Digital Set to Surpass TV in Time Spent with US Media." *eMarketer*. N.p., 1 Aug. 2013. Web. 03 Nov. 2013. <http://www.emarketer.com/m/Article/Digital-Set-Surpass-TV-Time-Spent-with-US-Media/1010096>.
5. Bounds, E. M. *Complete Works of E. M. Bounds*. Radford, VA: Wilder Publications, Limi, 2008. Print.
6. Yonggi Cho, David. *Prayer That Brings Revival*. Lake Mary, FL: Creation House, 1998. Print.
7. Sumrall, Lester. *Pioneers of Faith*. Tulsa, OK: Harrison House, 1995. Print.
8. Bonnke, Reinhard. "CfaN Firesite: Christ for All Nations' Online Community" CfaN Firesite: Christ for All Nations' Online Community: Crusade Index Page. N.p., n.d. Web. 04 July 2014. <http://support.cfan.org/site/PageServer?pagename=FSV2_Crusade_Index>.

9. Daly, Mary C., Daniel J. Wilson, and Norman J. Johnson. "Relative Status and Well-Being: Evidence from U.S. Suicide Deaths." *Review of Economics and Statistics* 95.5 (2013): 1480-500. Federal Reserve Bank of San Francisco. Web. 8 July 2014. <http://www.frbsf.org/economic-research/files/wp12-16bk.pdf>

10. Kiyosaki, Robert T., and Sharon L. Lechter. *Rich Dad, Poor Dad.* New York: Warner Business, 2000. Print.

11. Blum, Ron (April 10, 2009.) "New $1.5 Billion Yankee Stadium Formally Opens". *Yahoo! Sports.* Associated Press. Web. 9 July 2014. <http://en.wikipedia.org/wiki/Yankee_Stadium>.

12. "Intoxicated." Def. 1. Oxford Dictionaries. N.p., n.d. Web. <http://www.oxforddictionaries.com/us/definition/american_english/intoxicate?q=intoxicated>.

13. Raison, Charles. "Can Depression Cause Inability to Focus." *CNN.* N.p., 21 June 2011. Web. 29 July 2014. <http://thechart.blogs.cnn.com/2011/06/21/can-depression-cause-inability-to-focus/>.

14. "Facts & Statistics | Anxiety and Depression Association of America, ADAA." *Anxiety and Depression Association of America, ADAA.* ADAA, n.d. Web. 30 June 2013. <http://www.adaa.org/about-adaa/press-room/facts-statistics>.

15. McGhee, Paul E. *Health, Healing and the Amuse System: Humor as Survival Training.* Dubuque, IA: Kendall/Hunt, 1996. Print.

16. Bosworth, F. F. *Christ the Healer.* Old Tappan, NJ: F.H. Revell, 1973. Print.

ABOUT THE AUTHOR

TED SHUTTLESWORTH JR. has been involved in full-time ministry since he was a child. He began traveling on the road with his father and mother at the age of two weeks old. Five years later in a small church in Northern Maine, Ted felt the call of God on his life.

Ted has been preaching the gospel for close to two decades. As a third-generation minister, the responsibility to reap this end-time harvest of souls has been ingrained in him since childhood. The focus of Miracle Word Ministries is to preach the Word of God, see the Salvation of the Lord, and bring the miraculous power of Jesus Christ to a hungry generation.

Ted is a graduate of Rhema Bible Training College and currently resides in Virginia Beach, Virginia, with his wife, Carolyn, and their daughters Madelyn and Brooklyn. *Praise. Laugh. Repeat.* is his first book.

PRAYER OF SALVATION

Heavenly Father,

Thank you for sending your Son, Jesus, to die for me. I believe that You raised Him from the dead and that He is coming back soon.

I'm asking you to forgive me of my sin and make me brand new. Give me holy desires to pray and read your Word. Empower me by Your Holy Spirit to live for You for the rest of my life.

You are the Lord of my life. I thank you that the old life is gone and a new life has begun, in Jesus Name, Amen.

If you prayed this prayer, please contact us. We would like to send you a free gift, pray for you and help you take your next steps in Christ.

info@miracleword.co

Made in the USA
Middletown, DE
05 October 2015